TEACHING
WALKTHRUs

FIVE-STEP GUIDES TO INSTRUCTIONAL COACHING

TOM SHERRINGTON

& **OLIVER CAVIGLIOLI**

First published 2020

by John Catt Educational Ltd,
15 Riduna Park, Station Road,
Melton, Woodbridge IP12 1QT

Tel: +44 (0) 1394 389850
Email: enquiries@johncatt.com
Website: www.johncatt.com

ISBN: 978 1 912906 76 5

Typeset by John Catt Educational Limited

QUOTES

DYLAN WILIAM

Teaching WalkThrus is billed as 'a guide to instructional coaching' and of course, as you would expect from something produced by Tom Sherrington and Oliver Caviglioli, it is certainly an excellent resource for that purpose. But it is also much much more. It is a beautifully illustrated tour of the most important things to be thinking about in teaching, and in the leadership of teaching. Teaching is such a complex endeavour that the idea of a complete guide to teaching excellence is surely impossible, but this comes closer than anything I have seen to date. Anyone seriously interested in improving education needs this at their side.

SONIA THOMPSON

This pedagogical and practical manual is without a doubt what heads like me have been looking for. These two influential writers have created a visually stunning book for educationalists at all levels. For me, *Walkthrus* is a timely and welcome addition to our leadership armoury.

MARY MYATT

Utterly gripping and so clever to get to the heart of deep processes in such a lucid way both in words and images. The WalkThrus meet a real need because they bridge the gaps between, on the one hand, what we currently have strong evidence for in terms of developing pupils' learning and, on the other hand, precise guidance on how this might be brought to life in daily practice. A real feat and a great boon to the profession.

JOHN TOMSETT

WalkThrus gives us some of the key processes of teaching broken down into foolproof chunks. It is essential reading for anyone, at any stage of their career, who wants to improve their practice. I absolutely love it!

CRAIG BARTON

I've never seen anything quite like this before. This is not only a beautiful book, but an incredibly useful one. Powerful strategies brought to life by concise descriptions and clear images. Brilliant!

ROB COE

I love this book. If you want a practical and straight-out-of-the-box usable guide to specific classroom practices that are grounded in evidence, you'll love it too. The authors are two experienced and thoughtful former teachers, both of whom are genuine experts in their knowledge of the research that underpins classroom practice. Perhaps more importantly, they have plenty of experience of working with other teachers in a collaborative and supportive way to help them improve their classroom skills and effectiveness. *Teaching WalkThrus* is sure to become a much-valued classic.

ABOUT THE AUTHORS

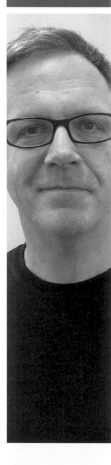

TOM SHERRINGTON

Tom started out as a physics and maths teacher in the 1980s and has since worked in numerous schools of different kinds as a teacher and leader, gathering ideas and working with a fabulous range of teachers and students.

He began writing the popular blog teacherhead.com as a way of sharing ideas and, encouraged by the engagement from teachers, went on to publish *The Learning Rainforest*, *Great Teaching in Real Classrooms* and *Rosenshine's Principles in Action*, working with Oliver and John Catt Ltd in both cases.

He works with schools and colleges providing support on curriculum, assessment and improving the quality of teaching and is a regular speaker and contributor to conferences and education festivals. Tom and Oliver are big fans of the researchED movement.

OLIVER CAVIGLIOLI

Oliver's childhood was steeped in design, thanks to his architect father's daily sermons on 'good taste'. His adulthood was immersed in the world of special schools, culminating in a decade of headship.

During that time, both backgrounds merged in the development of effective visual communication — firstly for children, then increasingly for colleagues.

Then, after a decade of training and writing about visual learning strategies, Oliver started illustrating other people's education books. In turn, that moved on to designing the structure, look and layout of the pages themselves.

His work with the Learning Scientists (*Understanding How We Learn*) was his first fully designed creation, soon followed by his own *Dual Coding With Teachers*. Previous collaboration with Tom Sherrington (both *Rainforest* books and *Rosenshine's Principles in Action*) meant that *Teaching WalkThrus* was a natural development. Here it is.

INTRODUCTION

Teaching WalkThrus came to life when we realised that there was growing interest in the elements that have informed our recent individual and collaborative projects. More teachers are looking to develop their practice harnessing the ideas from cognitive science and other areas of research. Both of us contribute to researchED conferences regularly and have experienced the rising demand for more information and guidance in an accessible form. School leaders are increasingly recognising the need for more finely tuned professional learning systems and content; they are seeing the limitations of top-down observation and feedback systems and the value of instructional coaching processes as an alternative is on the rise. The combination of visual images complementing technical professional guidance in short accessible resources has proved to be popular. All of these threads are woven together in WalkThrus which proved to be an extremely rewarding creative process for both of us.

Our first set of 50 WalkThru strategies is presented in three sections:

WHY? explores the reasons behind using visual guides to support teacher development alongside a selection of the key ideas from influential educational thinkers and researchers.

WHAT? comprises the 50 strategies organised into six sections covering the range of activities that teachers need to explore with any class. We selected a core collection to provide good coverage of common issues and practices based on the common themes that emerge from our discussions with teachers and school leaders. There will be more to come in future editions and formats.

HOW? includes a set of guides for teachers and leaders regarding the implementation of WalkThrus as a tool for teacher development. This includes the use of a WalkThru in an instructional coaching scenario and the more general organisation of effective professional learning. It also includes the A|D|A|P|T strategy that is central to our thinking. WalkThrus are written to be deliberately generic and context free so that anyone can use them. In the bottom-right of every WalkThru page you will find Attempt: Develop: Adapt: Practise: Test — spelling out ADAPT. It is essential the teachers ADAPT the steps so that they take form in their very specific contexts — with their subject; their students; their classroom.

We would like to acknowledge the support of Alex Sharratt and the John Catt team; our families for their support and encouragement; and, most of all, the researchers and teachers whose insights and enthusiasm for education have given us so much inspiration over the years.

Oliver and Tom

CONTENTS

WHY?

REASONS FOR THE WALKTHRUs

01

It is important that everyone involved in sharing ideas about teaching understands the underlying rationale and evidence base, where one exists. This applies to all of the ideas we explore in this book including the use of WalkThrus themselves. The Why section explores the reasons behind using visual guides to support teacher development alongside a selection of the key ideas from influential educational thinkers and researchers.

SECTIONS: **WHY?** | WHAT? | HOW?

10 | **CURATING TECHNIQUES** | WALKTHRUs | VISUAL
INSTRUCTIONS | DESIGN | SHARED UNDERSTANDING |
ROSENSHINE | WILLINGHAM | MARGE | WILIAM | BERGER |

CURATING TECHNIQUES

Teaching has made great strides in developing its professionalism in recent years. But despite the researchED movement and schools' adoption of evidence-based methods, teachers are still without ready access to a curated and designed collection of what we think are its best techniques.

This catalogue heralds a change. Gathered from research papers, reviews, books and daily practice, these WalkThru visual guides take teachers through each technique in consistent step-by-step clarity.

By building this index of excellence, we celebrate the practicality of research and the ingenuity of teachers.

PROFESSIONAL AMNESIA

Not only do fads come and go, so do well-researched, effective strategies. Retrieval practice and dual coding — to take just two examples — were everyday approaches in schools just a few decades ago. To many of today's teachers, they may well appear to be new. But in reality, they are once-forgotten and now rediscovered.

This professional amnesia thwarts attempts to build on past knowledge. Destructive loops of forgetting and rediscovery frustrate and demoralise teachers. If teachers are to be proud of their professionalism, surely they need to feel secure that classroom excellence is known, agreed, remembered and readily available?

Can there be any reasonable argument for not providing every teacher with 24/7 access to such a compilation of the best of the profession's practices? In which other profession, are its members left to discover for themselves — mostly in their own time — how to be excellent? Sure, we have plenty of narratives and opinions in books, policies and blogs but where is the 'technical manual'? Here it is, in dual coded format.

LETHAL MUTATION

This term, adopted by Dylan Wiliam, describes the sadly commonplace process whereby teachers learn a new technique from a course or book, adopt and adapt it for their practice. Then pass it on to colleagues. In such a linear, word-of-mouth fashion, there are inevitable mutations along the way. And, crucially, according to Wiliam, they tend to destroy the very aspects of the techniques that produced its effectiveness.

This deterioration of the technique's integrity is accelerated by the interpretation each individual has to make as they transform the verbal (text or spoken) description into their own private schema.

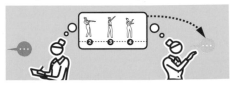

THE CHECKLIST MANIFESTO

Atul Gawande's analysis of how companies develop their staff identified a toxic pattern constructed around the notion of 'star quality'. Believing only some people were talented in this way, resulted in wasted effort in spotting it and a fierce guardianship by the anointed stars of their secret know–how.

Those companies who recognised the deluded and inefficient nature of this situation, started the job of pinpointing the essential steps involved in the 'star quality' behaviours. Checklists were built around these discoveries.

The WalkThrus are a form of checklists but not of the inflexible type. They put into step-by-step sequences, the actions needed for every teacher to execute 'star quality'. In doing so, we actively reject the sometimes lazy misreading of Polanyi that teaching contains so much 'tacit knowledge' that it's hopeless to be able to communicate any of it for the purpose of individual teacher development.

THE HUB, CONTEXT-FREE, MODEL

By making the WalkThrus context-free , they become a hub around which an orbit of teachers of different subjects and age phases can — indeed need to —add their own specific contexts. It is the ideal balance between a pessimistic view that teaching is an art that can't be communicated, and the overly optimistic behavioural checklists that over–specify teacher actions.

With the wide range of teachers relating to a single, context-free model, meaningful communication between them is supported by their shared understanding of the steps involved. So while the current focus on curriculum development rightly examines and asserts the individual nature of each subject, we mustn't ignore that teachers share much in terms of their classroom practice.

LINEAR MODEL

Due to the very structure of a linear model, it fosters a distortion and diminution of the original technique. Each recipient of the communication omits some aspect and adds others not originally there. Such repeated interpretations result in the lethal mutation that triggers constant change.

HUB MODEL

A hub model, by contrast, holds a context-free version at its centre. This both retains a consistent reference point and forces each adoption to be fashioned to a real context.

KS2 History context

KS4 Science context

As a result, teachers of different subjects, and from different age phases, can use their shared understanding of the central model to communicate and learn from each other.

SECTIONS: **WHY?** | **WHAT?** | **HOW?**

12   CURATING TECHNIQUES | **WALKTHRUs** | VISUAL
INSTRUCTIONS | DESIGN | SHARED UNDERSTANDING |
ROSENSHINE | WILLINGHAM | MARGE | WILIAM | BERGER |

WALKTHRUs

Verbal descriptions of teaching techniques are mostly too vague and, so, require too much guessing.

Videos contain too much irrelevant detail , obscuring the essentials of what makes a technique work well.

WalkThrus use both words and static images. Their design is based on clear decisions about what matters and what should be left out. As a result, they make teaching know-how as accessible — and attractive — as possible. They shorten the route to understanding.

By making expert pedagogy clear and concise, they democratise classroom expertise. Every teacher and organisation can improve their practice with WalkThrus.

Each WalkThru has 5 visual steps with a text description of the teacher's actions and thoughts.

STEP 1

STEP 2

STEP 3

STEP 4

STEP 5

DOUG LEMOV
2012

"Taking the time to preview and to prepare learners for what they should be looking for.

FLORENCE NIGHTINGALE
1858

"To affect thro' the eyes what we fail to convey to the public through their word-proof ears.

MICHAEL GRINDER
2000

"When the content is volatile, the communicator wants to display the information visually — the third point.

BARBARA TVERSKY
2019

"Aerial photographs don't make good maps … Include only the information that's useful for the task.

ATHAN N. AMASIATU
2013

"You can also use mental imagery to learn new routines, plays, or patterns.

CHARLOTTE E. WOLFF
2016

"Expert teachers attend to different facts and interpret information differently than novices.

JOHN SWELLER
2011

"Transience is a particular characteristic of dynamic representations that has ramifications for working memory load.

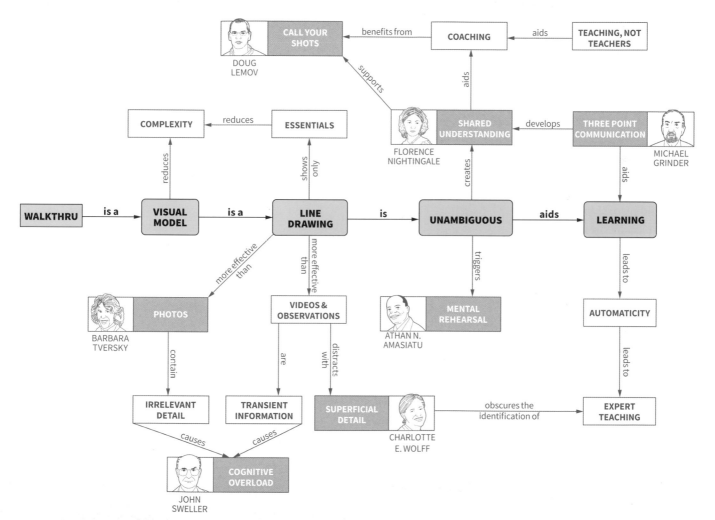

SECTIONS: **WHY?** | WHAT? | HOW?

14 | CURATING TECHNIQUES | WALKTHRUs | **VISUAL INSTRUCTIONS** | DESIGN | SHARED UNDERSTANDING | ROSENSHINE | WILLINGHAM | MARGE | WILIAM | BERGER |

VISUAL INSTRUCTIONS

Pope Gregory I (540–604) once declared that pictures were for those who couldn't read. But by the Middle Ages, diagrams had become essential for the building of ships, churches and windmills. Medical manuals directed doctors to which parts of the body were suitable for cauterising.

In 1751 , Diderot and D'Alembert — kicking off the Enlightenment — produced *La Grande Encyclopédie* with 600 pages of illustrated instructions. Their intention? To *"remove the secrecy from craft traditions"* (Mijksenaar & Westendorp 1999). While teaching expertise is not a secret, its manoeuvres , however, could do with a bit more clarification in text and images.

GO

EXPLAIN NOT JUST SHOW

Professor Barbara Tversky, author of *Mind In Motion* (2019) and over two hundred articles on memory, spatial thinking and design, has much wisdom to share on instructional design.

She reminds us that *"animations just show, they don't explain"* as well as moving too quickly to make sense of what's going on. And that *"it's a short hop from describing events step-by-step to creating instructions to do them"*.

BARBARA TVERSKY

Include only the information that's useful for the task … exaggerate, even distort, the useful information to make it easy to find and follow.

CATEGORIES OF INSTRUCTIONS

According to Paul Mijksenaar and Piet Westendorp (1999) in their comprehensive survey of instructional design, there are eleven categories into which they fit.

Warnings: A red X, a hand stop sign or an exclamation mark are hall marks.

Identification: For new technology, this is essential — which parts do what?

Measurements: Calibrations of both time and space for essential accuracy.

Composition: When putting things together, it's critical to know how the parts fit.

Location and Orientation: Fundamental to DIY is knowing where the parts connect.

Sequences: Often shown movie-style in storyboards (e.g. these WalkThrus).

Movements: Verbs often depicted with elaborate interplay of arrows.

Connections: Arrows again, joining parts together.

Action: Verbs and precise positions combine to clarify what to do.

Cause and Effect: Pinpointing the link between action and reaction (effect).

That's What It Should Look Like: The end, desired, result of a series of actions.

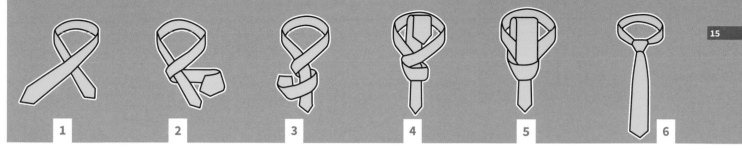

1   2   3   4   5   6

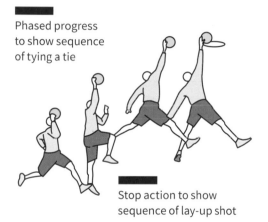

Phased progress to show sequence of tying a tie

Stop action to show sequence of lay-up shot

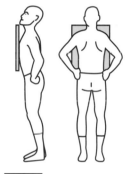

Two perspectives to show X-ray instructions

Superimposed angle to show correct gait

Lighter colour to show next move

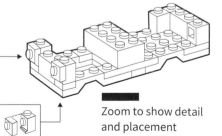

Zoom to show detail and placement

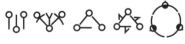

Notation to show placement in synchronised swimming

Arrows to show direction of dumbbells

SECTIONS: WHY? | WHAT? | HOW?

16 CURATING TECHNIQUES | WALKTHRUs | VISUAL
INSTRUCTIONS | DESIGN | SHARED UNDERSTANDING |
ROSENSHINE | WILLINGHAM | MARGE | WILIAM | BERGER |

DESIGN

Design is more than decoration. At *The Guardian* newspaper offices, the designers over the last decade have moved from a basement office to being in the main editorial hub. Graphic design, in all its aspects, is central in the conceiving and creating process.

So, too, in education. The busy contemporary teacher wants to find information easily without having to work hard to identify key points. They also want the information to be attractively designed — to reflect the status of a modern profession. And, above all, they want the principles of cognitive science to be obviously applied. The publication has to clearly 'walk the talk'.

THE PROBLEM WITH VIDEO

Video has disappointed. John Sweller, the cognitive load guru, reports that video hasn't achieved its once hoped-for potential for learning (Sweller et al 2011).Moving at the speed of life, video suffers from the transient information effect, whereby viewers have to store rapidly disappearing images in their working memory.

Furthermore, videos of teachers in the classroom contain so much surface distracting information — the furniture, the clothing, the displays — that they obscure the learning points. Indeed John Bransford (Bransford et al 2000) doubts that anyone but an expert is able to accurately perceive the significant action points when observing a teacher, live or through video. So, what about still photographs then?

WHY PHOTOGRAPHS DON'T WORK

Alberto Cairo, practitioner and professor of graphic communication, reminds us that *"a photograph includes too much information that's irrelevant for understanding what's going on"* (Cairo 2013). Verisimilitude, it seems, isn't all it's cracked up to be.

LINE DRAWINGS CLARIFY

A fascinating aspect of our perception is that we identify objects by their external boundaries, not by their internal characteristics. So, adding shading, texture, and other such surface details is not only unnecessary, it adds to the visual 'noise'.

Borrowed from physics, the notion of the signal-to-noise ratio helps designers explain why such additional details detract from the intended message (the signal). For this reason, not only are the WalkThru figures stylised, they also have no textural qualities. And to further clarify the signal, there is no background classroom detail such as desks, boards, even chairs.

WORKING MEMORY CONSIDERATIONS

Most WalkThrus are processes, with a start, middle and end. A natural flow chart, organised from left to right for a familiar reading habit. Steps are limited to five, consistent with Cowan's research (Cowan 2001) on working memory capacity when dealing with meaningful content (4 plus or minus 1). And to establish consistency, the five-step approach is applied to all WalkThrus, across all the series.

THE STICK FIGURE

The modern graphic stick figure starts with Otto Neurath and his illustrator, Gerd Arntz in the 1930s. Rudolf Modley converted them into stylish clip art in the 1970s, as below.

Otl Aicher brilliantly stylised the stick figure in 1972 for the Munich Olympic Games.

Xplane, the US visual communications company, adapted the figure for the modern office in the 2000s.

Our everyday reminder of this graphic approach is, of course, the toilet sign.

Non realistic depiction of concepts

Signalling a gesture

Non realistic platforms and titles to signal messages

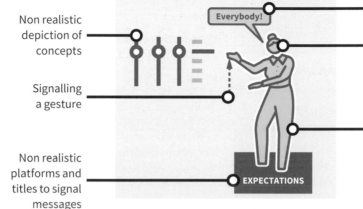

Everybody!

EXPECTATIONS

Sometimes, words will be in speech bubbles

Generic teachers — one female, one male, who we refer to as Chloe and Chuka

Stylised bodies with minimal details but still with charm

Each series has a different colour background

Most speech bubbles simply indicate speech content

Each series has a different colour combination of teachers

SOPHISTICATED
APPROPRIATE
ACCURATE

EXPLORE DIFFERENCES

Concept names can be part of the image

Symbols to show degrees of quality

An extra white border line to contrast the image against a background

SECTIONS: **WHY?** | WHAT? | HOW?

18 CURATING TECHNIQUES | WALKTHRUs | VISUAL
INSTRUCTIONS | DESIGN | **SHARED UNDERSTANDING** |
ROSENSHINE | WILLINGHAM | MARGE | WILIAM | BERGER |

SHARED UNDERSTANDING

Studies reveal just how ineffective professional development can often be. Much of this analysis is based on an organisational or systems focus. But less attention is paid to the individual teacher psychology — the sort of cognitive science focus that illuminates student learning.

WalkThrus provide the psychology that helps establish an embodied understanding of the technique, as well as a communication dynamic that develops this into a shared perception.

In the potentially delicate situation of giving and receiving feedback — think coaching and observations — WalkThrus offer an ingenious solution that builds rather than diminishes trust.

THREE POINT COMMUNICATION

Feedback is an important part of learning. Especially when the execution of a skill is involved. However, it remains a difficult conversation to execute, despite our best intentions. Because, contrary to our intuition and customary advice, a face-to-face dynamic is at fault.

Everyone is looking down and checking what it says. Interactions are therefore object-centred and not person-centred.

ERIC LUNZER

Directing feedback at a colleague will invariably trigger personal feelings and private responses. But, by both people sitting side-by-side, they can look at a shared visual focus (the WalkThru) and direct their comments to each other through it. Immediately the tone changes, becoming more friendly. That desired level of objectivity required for effective feedback is far more easily achieved in this dynamic.

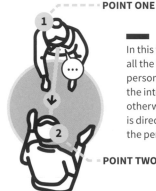

POINT ONE

POINT TWO

In this typical situation all the feedback is personal, despite the intention to be otherwise — because it is directed squarely to the person's face.

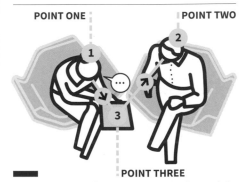

POINT ONE   **POINT TWO**

POINT THREE

In this dynamic, all communication is directed via a third point — the shared visual. There is now a gap between the messenger and their message. Comments are now about the teaching and not the teacher.

SHARED UNDERSTANDING

The principles of Three Point Communication also apply when in group situations. Externalising ideas in a public domain shapes communication, often avoiding many of the political games people play. By directing comments to the visual itself, overly subjective reactions can be by-passed. Consequently, instead of each individual pivoting their thinking around their own private — and often unexamined — interpretations, a visual provides a focus that unites the thinking of each member of the group. A tangible sense of a team understanding is rapidly established.

NANCY DUARTE

A presentation that creates common ground has the potential to unite a diverse group of people toward a common purpose.

MICHAEL GRINDER

When the content is volatile, the communicator wants to display the information visually — the third point.

In his book *Visual Teams*, David Sibbert emphasises the significance of building fellowship. At times when initiatives and innovations abound, individuals can often flounder in attempting to make sense of this explosion of information. Creating a team understanding at these very times, is an antidote to such fragmentation. People don't need merely to hear or read about visions, they need to see them.

Such a common focus and perception has significant benefits when applied to coaching and observations situations. When the context is technical — as is Instructional Coaching — it is essential. In the later How? section of this book, you can study a five-step WalkThru process called **Observations** that shows you how to apply these principles in action.

INDIVIDUAL LEARNING

Our bodies, it seems, find it hard to distinguish between real and imagined experiences. Barbara Tversky (2019) reports that viewing actions or depictions of actions stimulate the viewer in having muscular responses.

Following the storyboard structure of the WalkThrus can give viewers a sense of the visceral feel of enacting the illustrated behaviours. This provides a serious head start in learning and absorbing the actions that compose the technique.

Cognitive psychologists Fiorella and Mayer have written a book on the power of generative learning (2015). They define it as occurring when learners *"actively make sense of the material so they can apply their learning to new situations"*.

By making the WalkThrus context–free, viewers are nudged to imagine their own classroom situation in the vacuum. It is this act of creating a familiar scene in one's mind's eye that initiates a mental rehearsal. In this respect, it resembles the pre–match psychological preparation of sports people.

SECTIONS: **WHY?** | WHAT? | HOW?

20

CURATING TECHNIQUES | WALKTHRUs | VISUAL
INSTRUCTIONS | DESIGN | SHARED UNDERSTANDING |
ROSENSHINE | WILLINGHAM | MARGE | WILIAM | BERGER |

ROSENSHINE'S PRINCIPLES OF INSTRUCTION
STRANDS 1 & 2

In 2010, Barak Rosenshine published a set of 10 Principles of Instruction based on evidence from cognitive science, research into the classroom practices of 'master teachers' and into various cognitive supports such as scaffolding and reading aloud.

He suggests that there is 'no conflict at all' between the instructional suggestions that come from these types of research. We have organised his 10 principles into four strands as per Tom's popular 'Principles in Action' book, so the numbering here does not match Rosenshine's original.

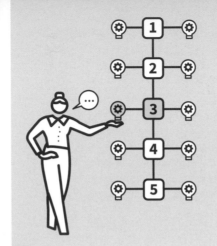

1

PRESENT NEW MATERIAL USING SMALL STEPS

Break down the curriculum section you are teaching as suggested in **Sequence Concepts in Small Steps**. The size of the steps that you introduce at once will depend on the level of students' prior knowledge and confidence. Rosenshine suggests that more effective teachers tend to spend more time providing explanations, modelling and guiding practice at each stage. Make sure you are not asking students to practise too many steps at once. Build confidence, step by step.

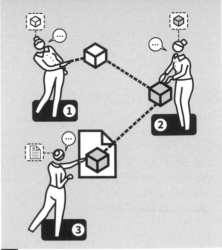

2

PROVIDE MODELS

Rosenshine suggests that modelling, with the teacher thinking aloud as they demonstrate how to tackle a task, is an example of the cognitive support students need. **Worked Examples & Backward Fading** are an important form of this; a step-by-step demonstration of what to do, reinforcing the underlying principles followed by student practice with partially completed examples. Other ideas are covered in **Live Modelling** and **Set the Standards**.

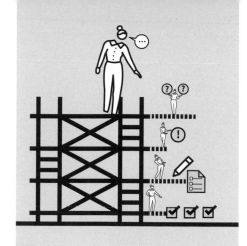

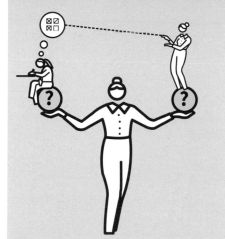

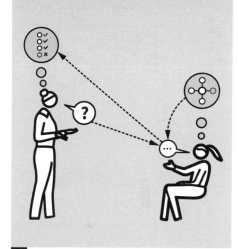

PROVIDE SCAFFOLDS FOR DIFFICULT TASKS

This is explored in the WalkThru **Scaffolding**. Rosenshine suggests effective teachers engage students in a 'cognitive apprenticeship', supporting them to reach ambitious goals using scaffolding processes that guide them on the way. The metaphor of 'scaffolding' embeds the idea that, when ready, the supports are withdrawn. Scaffolding is only temporary and must not become relied upon in the long run. Scaffolds include modelling, checklists and writing frames and anticipating errors and misconceptions.

ASK QUESTIONS

Rosenshine highlights the dual purpose of questions:

a) to provide opportunities for student practice

b) to allow a teacher to determine how well material has been learned, informing their decision to move on or to provide additional instruction. His review of research suggests that when teachers ask more questions, involving all students, their learning outcomes improve. We have devoted several WalkThrus to specific questioning techniques in the section **Questioning and Feedback**.

CHECK FOR STUDENT UNDERSTANDING

Rosenshine places significant emphasis on the importance of this process as covered in the WalkThru **Check for Understanding**. Importantly it takes the form of asking questions such as 'what have you understood?' and not the rhetorical 'have you understood?'. The process has two deep outcomes:

a) it allows students to elaborate their thinking, augmenting connections between different ideas and concepts, deepening their understanding

b) it alerts the teacher to aspects of the material that might need to be re-taught.

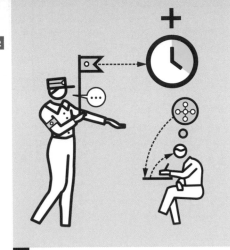

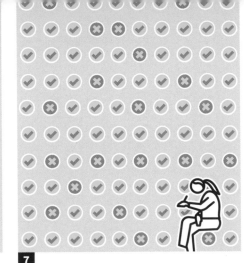

6

GUIDE STUDENT PRACTICE

This principle is explored in our WalkThru **Guided Practice**. Rosenshine's paper suggests that teachers who spend more time in guided practice will secure higher success rates from students. This involves involving students in practising applying or elaborating material in small steps with the teacher asking questions, checking for understanding and checking for errors. If guided practice is too short, students often make more errors in independent practice.

7

OBTAIN A HIGH SUCCESS RATE

Rosenshine tells us that research indicates an optimal success rate for student achievement at around 80%. This provides the best balance of successful practice and consolidation and appropriate level of challenge. If students are asked to practise too much material at once and begin to make errors, they are more likely to form misconceptions. It is important to stop and re-teach material where students are not succeeding or to adjust the level of challenge. If the success rate is much higher than 80%, the work might be too easy.

8

INDEPENDENT PRACTICE

This principle is covered in our WalkThru **Independent Practice**. Overlearning from independent practice is essential for student fluency and automaticity in using a skill or applying knowledge. Fluency is an important element in learning as it frees up working memory. It's vital that independent practice builds on successful guided practice so students are truly consolidating and not floundering. More confident students can progress to this stage more rapidly. **Collaborative Learning** and other ideas from **Mode B Teaching** can be useful forms of independent practice.

SECTIONS: **WHY?** | WHAT? | HOW?

CURATING TECHNIQUES | WALKTHRUs | VISUAL INSTRUCTIONS | DESIGN | SHARED UNDERSTANDING | **ROSENSHINE** | WILLINGHAM | MARGE | WILIAM | BERGER |

23

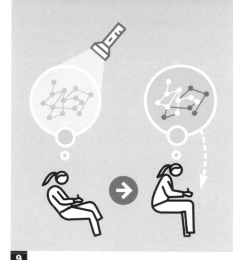

9

DAILY REVIEW

Rosenshine begins with this principle because it is a good idea to engage students in a review of prior learning before building on it with new related material. There are numerous methods of doing this that involve all students exploring their schema for the knowledge at hand, helping them make stronger connections, gain fluency and for teacher and students to identify gaps in recall. Strategies for doing this are explored in the **Weekly and Monthly Review** WalkThru and the whole **Practice and Retrieval** section.

10

WEEKLY AND MONTHLY REVIEW

The same techniques can be used as suggested for **Daily Review**. In this principle, Rosenshine emphasises the need for students to be involved in extensive practice to develop well-connected and automatic knowledge: *'the more one rehearses and reviews information, the stronger the interconnections between the materials become'*. Weekly and Monthly reviews also attend to the problem of forgetting; it's important to strike a balance between covering a lot of material and providing time for sufficient practice with each part.

ROSENSHINE'S PRINCIPLES OF INSTRUCTION
STRANDS 3 & 4

Continuing our summary of Rosenshine's Principles, it's important to stress that the 10 principles work well as a guide for personal reflection but not as a universal checklist or template for any single lesson. The principles are popular because they are grounded in the common daily practice of many teachers, with no element of faddishness. However, most teachers could still seek to improve their practice still further and we would encourage teachers to apply our ADAPT framework to each of the principles.

SECTIONS: **WHY?** | WHAT? | HOW?

24

CURATING TECHNIQUES | WALKTHRUs | VISUAL
INSTRUCTIONS | DESIGN | SHARED UNDERSTANDING |
ROSENSHINE | **WILLINGHAM** | MARGE | WILIAM | BERGER |

5 LESSONS FROM DAN WILLINGHAM'S *WHY DON'T STUDENTS LIKE SCHOOL?*

Published in 2009, this is arguably one of the most influential books on cognitive science and its implications for teachers that there is. Willingham takes ideas from the study of how we learn and applies it to several familiar challenges that teachers face.

His chapters 'Why do students forget everything I say?' and 'Why is it so hard for students to understand abstract ideas?' are at once insightful, practical and reassuring, linking theory to practice.

1

MEMORY IS THE RESIDUE OF THOUGHT

Willingham's famous phrase leads into a number of concrete suggestions. To get students to remember what we teach, we need to get them to think about the meaning of any new material in the context of what they already know. His main recommendation is: Review each lesson plan in terms of what the student is likely to think about. This means stripping out extraneous distractions and designing assignments so students will unavoidably think about the meaning of the content, not merely observe it or move it around.

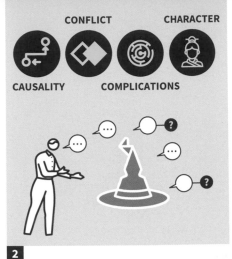

2

THE POWER OF STORIES

Willingham suggests 'the human mind seems exquisitely tuned to understand and remember stories'. Stories contain the four Cs: *causality, conflict, complications and character*. Stories help with learning because students understand their structure and will fill in gaps, they are interesting and they are easy to remember, aided by their causal structure. The implication is to structure lessons, organising the material, in the way stories are structured using the four Cs.

3

UNDERSTANDING IS REMEMBERING IN DISGUISE

People often distinguish 'knowing' and 'understanding' but Willingham makes a strong case that, when we understand something, that is because we are able to bring forward ideas we already know from memory and make connections between them. The implication for developing understanding is to support students to recall relevant, largely concrete ideas they already know and to provide new examples, so they can be compared, combined or manipulated to foster understanding. This links to the **Abstract models with Concrete Examples** WalkThru.

SHALLOW TO DEEP

4

DEEP KNOWLEDGE THE GOAL; SHALLOW KNOWLEDGE COMES FIRST

Willingham explains how acquiring shallow knowledge — individual facts and ideas — is often a necessary preliminary stage on the road to deep knowledge, where more extensive connections can be made. However there's a risk of allowing students to stop at the shallow stage unless we continually make the deeper knowledge goals explicit. At the same time, teachers need to be realistic and accept that the deeper connections can take years to form. Meanwhile, shallow knowledge is a good start. It's important.

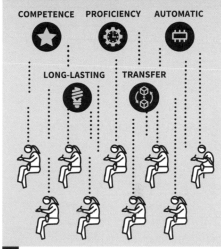

5

IS DRILLING WORTH IT? THE POWER OF PRACTICE

Willingham highlights several benefits of practice:
Gaining minimum competence to perform a task. | Improving proficiency in a task. | Helping a memory process become automatic. | Making memory long lasting Increasing the likelihood of transfer to new situations.
He suggests we prioritise practising with knowledge students need to become automatic; space out the practice returning to material repeatedly over time and fold practice into more advanced skills to add interest and depth.

SECTIONS: **WHY?** | WHAT? | HOW?

26 CURATING TECHNIQUES | WALKTHRUs | VISUAL INSTRUCTIONS | DESIGN | SHARED UNDERSTANDING | ROSENSHINE | WILLINGHAM | **MARGE** | WILIAM | BERGER |

SHIMAMURA'S MARGE MODEL

Published as a free online e-book in 2018, Shimamura's *A Whole-Brain Learning Approach for Students and Teachers* introduces the MARGE acronym. Each element leads to practical suggestions for any teacher dealing with conceptual learning, underpinned by fascinating insights from cognitive science. A key idea is that we don't 'soak up' learning; it requires 'top down processing' whereby we actively use existing knowledge to guide and select relevant information.

1

MOTIVATE

Given the range of distractions and effort required, it's important to support students to generate the mental motivation to focus on the material in hand. This can be done by:

- Stimulating curiosity, framing learning through big questions and links to an overarching schema
- Harnessing story-telling: what will happen next?
- The aesthetic question: engaging students' emotional responses and personal views.
- Exploring new places, visiting museums, field trips.

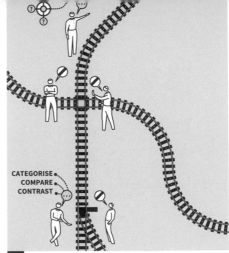

2

ATTEND

Studies show that mind-wandering is rampant; it's natural and predictable. Teachers can generate and sustain attention by:

- Asking questions that make the learning goals explicit at the start of a session
- Chunking information into small pieces
- The 3 Cs: *categorise, compare, contrast* — linking new ideas to existing ones.
- Taking stock of learning at key points in a lesson, encouraging students in thinking about the material.

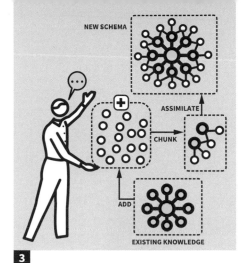

3

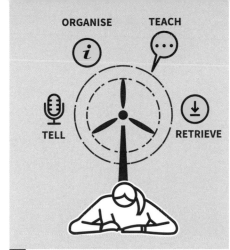

4

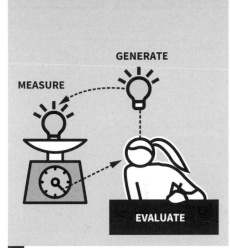

5

RELATE

We build secure memory by actively and repeatedly relating new information to what we already know. Teachers can support students in this process by:

- Asking students to chunk up information, grouping it into meaningful related sets of ideas
- Using visual imagery, metaphors and analogies linking ideas to prior knowledge
- Organising information into visual schematic representations or concept maps
- Applying the 3Cs, making mental movies and engaging in elaborative interrogation

GENERATE

Students need to actively self-generate information in working memory, not simply restating what has been learned but reframing it in their own terms. The more often students self-generate material, "*the better it will be established as a long-lasting memory*". Linking to the ideas of **Practice and Retrieval**, Shimamura suggests that students:

- Tell other students what they've learned
- Test themselves using the 3Cs with books closed
- Teach material to others
- Space practice, retrieving information in their own words

EVALUATE

It's essential for students to gain a true idea of their capacity to recall knowledge avoiding the illusion of familiarity. Using accurate resources to check their own knowledge against, repeated Generate-Evaluate cycles help students fill gaps in their knowledge. Ideas suggested include:

- Delaying testing by minutes or hours to be sure of evaluating ideas that have lodged in long-term memory
- Testing generatively, telling someone what has been learned
- Constructing and using flash cards
- Interleaving topics and testing repeatedly

SECTIONS: **WHY?** | WHAT? | HOW?

28

CURATING TECHNIQUES | WALKTHRUs | VISUAL
INSTRUCTIONS | DESIGN | SHARED UNDERSTANDING |
ROSENSHINE | WILLINGHAM | MARGE | **WILIAM** | BERGER |

WILIAM et al
FIVE FORMATIVE
ASSESSMENT STRATEGIES

In his book *Embedded Formative Assessment*, Dylan Wiliam explains the five key strategies devised by Leahy, Lyon, Thompson and Wiliam in 2005. These are all linked to the 'big idea' that teaching is *adaptive* to the learner's needs. Here we give a brief outline of each of the five formative assessment strategies.

As part of formative assessment, where students play a key role themselves, a teacher's role is to engage in 'responsive teaching' whereby their instructional inputs and interactions with students need to adapt and respond, depending on how the learning is going.

SIOBHÁN
LEAHY

CLARIFYING | UNDERSTANDING | SHARING
LEARNING INTENTIONS

1

CLARIFYING, UNDERSTANDING, AND SHARING LEARNING INTENTIONS

To get anywhere, it helps to know where we are going — in learning as in mapping a real journey. There is no simple formula but in general research shows that it helps to be explicit with students about what they should know and what the success criteria for judging quality might be. Crucially students need to understand intentions; it's not sufficient simply to be told them.

HINGE QUESTIONS

2

ENGINEERING EFFECTIVE CLASSROOM DISCUSSIONS, TASKS AND ACTIVITIES THAT ELICIT EVIDENCE OF LEARNING

In order to monitor where students are in their learning relative to the intentions, we need to elicit evidence. The main ways of doing this are through effective questioning including diagnostic and hinge-point questions, whole-class response methods and listening to discussions. Wiliam cites a range of techniques similar to those in **Questioning and Feedback**.

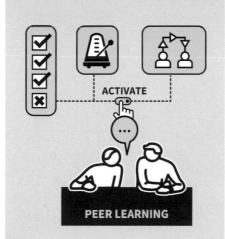

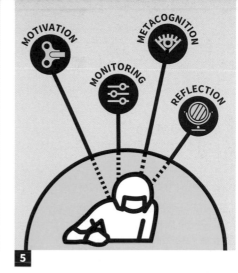

3

4

5

PROVIDING FEEDBACK THAT MOVES LEARNERS FORWARD

Feedback is complex and problematic so teachers need to think carefully about the responses that their specific individual students have to information they receive regarding their past performance.

Generally feedback should be:

- Designed to make students think — not generate an emotional response
- Focused on learning goals that have been shared
- More work for the student than the teacher, focusing on students owning the process.

ACTIVATING STUDENTS AS LEARNING RESOURCES FOR ONE ANOTHER

Collaborative Learning can be very powerful if deployed effectively. Well-structured activities give opportunities to:

a) provide peer assessment focused on improvement: checking answers, spotting errors, applying checklists for elements of assignments;

b) provide generative rehearsal via peer teaching opportunities whereby students teach things to each other, clarifying their own understanding in the process.

ACTIVATING STUDENTS AS OWNERS OF THEIR OWN LEARNING

Only learners create learning. Research shows that the better learners are able to manage their learning, the better they learn. This can be developed by attending to motivation, metacognition (as with Rosenshine's Process Questions), supporting students to check their own progress toward the shared learning intentions (as with self-quizzing) and to involve students in reflecting on their learning in a structured way.

SECTIONS: **WHY?** | WHAT? | HOW?

30

CURATING TECHNIQUES | WALKTHRUs | VISUAL
INSTRUCTIONS | DESIGN | SHARED UNDERSTANDING |
ROSENSHINE | WILLINGHAM | MARGE | WILIAM | **BERGER** |

RON BERGER'S ETHIC OF EXCELLENCE

Ron Berger is well-known for his excellent book *An Ethic of Excellence* and for his presentation of the Austin's Butterfly story — readily available via an internet search. His philosophy is powerful: "I believe that work of excellence is transformational … Once a student sees that he or she is capable of excellence, that student is never quite the same … they're never quite satisfied with less." His book sets out concrete steps we can take to establish a culture based on this ethic.

1

SELF-ESTEEM FROM ACCOMPLISHMENTS

Berger is clear that we can't first build students' self-esteem and then focus on their work: "*It is through their own work that self-esteem will grow.*" We do not help students by giving them compliments or protecting them from the truth; they will only be proud of themselves when they produce work they can value. This means our emphasis is positive but relentlessly strategic: how can we improve the work to make it excellent?

2

MODELS

A key element in Berger's approach is to provide students with models to emulate for the projects and tasks they undertake. It is legitimate for students to borrow or even copy ideas at the initial stages of learning. Models provide a reference point for discussing the detailed elements of excellent writing or art work and can extend to the behaviours and attitudes of students in their approach to their work. It's useful to have a wide range of models from current and former students as well as adult experts.

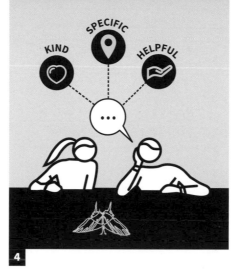

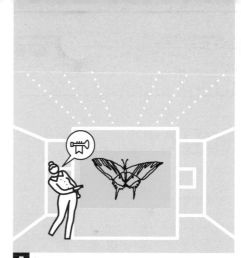

MULTIPLE DRAFTS

Berger asks: *"What could you produce of quality in a single draft?"* He suggests that students need to know from the outset that quality means rethinking, reworking and polishing. This brings some time management issues so it is important to have extended periods within which redrafting will take place with a clear deadline in mind — e.g. the date of the exhibition or performance. However, the path to excellence consists of making many iterative improvements so the opportunity for re-drafting is essential.

CRITIQUE

This method is modelled in Austin's Butterfly, where he is given feedback on his drawing by his peers. Berger's rules are:

- Be kind; the environment must feel safe; hurtful comments are unacceptable
- Be specific; comments must give actionable guidance. It's no good just saying 'it's good'.
- Be helpful; comments must move things forward so repeating previous suggestions or pointing out irrelevant faults just wastes time.

Ideally, critique focuses on the work, not the person, and involves them explaining their thinking.

MAKE WORK PUBLIC

Berger suggests that when students know their work will be displayed it takes on a different significance. You give them a reason to care about it. Making work public reinforces numerous messages about quality but also gives students a short-term reward for the effort they apply. This involves setting up regular exhibitions with invitations to visitors and opportunities to showcase the processes leading to the final products.

WHAT?

THE WALKTHRU SERIES

01

WHY?
REASONS FOR
THE WALKTHRUs
PAGE 08

02

03

HOW?
WALKTHRUS FOR
DEVELOPMENT
PAGE 150

In this book we have selected 50 ideas to present as WalkThrus. Our intention is to produce further sets in future editions and formats. Our WalkThru strategies are organised into six sections that cover the range of activities that teachers need to explore with any class. In each case we have selected a core selection of ideas to provide good coverage of common issues and practices based on the common themes that emerge from our discussions with teachers and school leaders. There is no intention for these to be regarded as an exhaustive or definitive set. Future editions will extend the range in each of the six areas.

BEHAVIOUR & RELATIONSHIPS

Establishing conditions for learning with positive relationships and secure routines

CURRICULUM PLANNING

Designing a great curriculum, rich in knowledge, experiences and challenge

EXPLAINING & MODELLING

Techniques for developing students' understanding, linking new ideas to what they know

QUESTIONING & FEEDBACK

Techniques for responsive teaching during lessons, asking questions and giving good feedback

PRACTICE & RETRIEVAL

Techniques for reinforcing students' understanding, building fluency and confidence

MODE B TEACHING

Exploring the possibilities for student learning with opportunities for independent learning and oracy

BEHAVIOUR AND RELATIONSHIPS

01

It's essential that teachers create an environment in which all students feel they belong and feel safe; an environment that allows all students to thrive as individuals and as learners. This requires establishing appropriate learning-focused relationships where expectations are set high and where everyone knows the routines and the boundaries. This collection of WalkThrus covers some basic ideas and techniques to support teachers in achieving this. The ADAPT concept will be important as circumstances will vary significantly from one setting to another.

POSITIVE RELATIONSHIPS
PAGE 36

Blending warmth, kindness and assertiveness

ESTABLISH YOUR EXPECTATIONS
PAGE 38

Setting and maintaining high expectations

SIGNAL, PAUSE, INSIST
PAGE 40

Gaining focused attention on a signal

POSITIVE FRAMING
PAGE 42

Creating a positive atmosphere through affirmative language.

REHEARSE ROUTINES
PAGE 44

Designing, rehearsing and reinforcing common class routines

CHOICES & CONSEQUENCES
PAGE 46

Using choices and consequences systems for excellent behaviour

SECTIONS: WHY? | **WHAT?** | HOW?

36 | BEHAVIOUR & RELATIONSHIPS | CURRICULUM PLANNING
EXPLAINING & MODELLING | QUESTIONING & FEEDBACK
PRACTICE & RETRIEVAL | MODE B TEACHING

POSITIVE RELATIONSHIPS

There are multiple reasons for teachers to establish positive relationships with students. Most importantly, relationships support the needs and rights of everyone in a classroom to feel safe, respected and valued; to feel they belong. Positive relationships also underpin creating conditions where students and teachers can focus on learning, free from distractions or emotional threats. Finally, positive relationships are key in communicating trustable feedback that students will act on. Importantly, in classrooms relationships are also inescapably aligned to the different roles and responsibilities that teachers and students have.

WALKTHRUs IN THIS SERIES

BEHAVIOUR & RELATIONSHIPS

1

ESTABLISH NORMS AROUND CLEAR ROLES AND BOUNDARIES

Make it explicit to students through your messages and interactions, that you as their teacher have responsibility for them and that this gives you role-authority alongside a duty of care. Adopt a mindset where your relationships with students focus on the shared purpose of achieving learning rather than on interpersonal connections. Once students understand the boundaries for positive, valued behaviours and that these are consistently and judiciously maintained, they accept them as norms within which everyone co-exists happily.

2

COMMUNICATE KINDNESS

If there's one thing that all positive relationships have in common, it is kindness. If you think about all of your students and classes through a lens of kindness, it influences all of your interactions, the things you say and the way you say them, the expectations you have of students and the way they interact with each other. Keep kindness at the forefront especially if you have challenging situations to deal with.

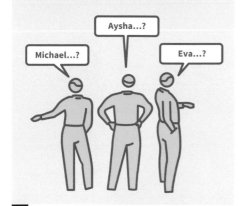

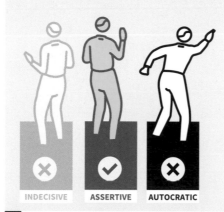

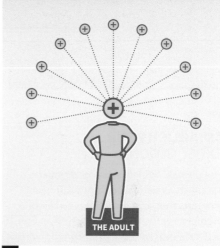

3

LEARN NAMES AND USE THEM

It is much easier to communicate warmth and kindness to students if you know their names. It pays to take time to learn names early on with a new class, using a seating plan, for example, to reference as you ask questions in the early stages. If you can say *"Michael, what do you think?"* or *"Aysha, let's have you facing this way, thanks"*, it's so much better than the alternatives when you do not know their name or say it incorrectly.

4

COMBINE ASSERTIVENESS WITH WARMTH

As Bill Rogers describes, the ideal demeanour for a teacher is one of being assertive, rather than autocratic or indecisive. Assertiveness involves expecting compliance with your expectations without using power to demand respect. It's possible to be very strict if needed, strongly enforcing a boundary, at the same time as being warm, kind and caring. Use a tone of voice and body language that is firm but warm or switches quickly from one to the other. Be firm when needed, consistently and fairly, whilst also communicating that students are valued and respected.

5

ALWAYS BE THE ADULT

This applies when you are challenged by students behaving inappropriately. However badly they behave, however inappropriate the language they might use, it is vital to remain as calm and rational as possible, taking a pause to compose yourself if necessary. Listen for the substance of what students are saying and respond using adult language and **Positive Framing**, maintaining a professional demeanour, without seeking to have the last word or resorting to sarcasm, idle threats or personal remarks.

SECTIONS: WHY? | **WHAT?** | HOW?

38 **BEHAVIOUR & RELATIONSHIPS** | CURRICULUM PLANNING
EXPLAINING & MODELLING | QUESTIONING & FEEDBACK
PRACTICE & RETRIEVAL | MODE B TEACHING

ESTABLISH YOUR EXPECTATIONS

The phrase 'you establish what you establish' is borrowed from Bill Rogers. It means that, if, in practice, you tolerate mediocre work, poor punctuality and off-task talking, you have established that this is the norm so this is what you will get. On the other hand, if you establish that you will not tolerate these things and will take actions to address them, students learn to function within those higher expectations. What ever you establish and sustain becomes the norm. Another version of this is the idea that 'what you permit, you promote'.

WALKTHRUs IN THIS SERIES

BEHAVIOUR & RELATIONSHIPS

1

DECIDE YOUR EXPECTATIONS

Ideally this will form part of a whole-school process or a team process, but within your own classroom you need to determine exactly what your expectations are for every aspect of running your lessons: the equipment that is expected, how to enter a room and move between one set of activities and another; how to listen when others are talking; how to ask and answer questions; how work should be set out. Before enforcing your expectations, work out exactly what they are in as much detail as possible.

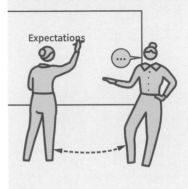

2

COMMUNICATE YOUR EXPECTATIONS

Take time to talk through your expectations with each class. It is helpful to write them down and use visual reminders that you can refer to for clarification. Use a **Checking for Understanding** process to ensure your students know what you mean. If you are unclear about your expectations, this will show in their responses later on. For some routines, it is important to walk through them, rehearsing how they will move or behave in a certain situation.

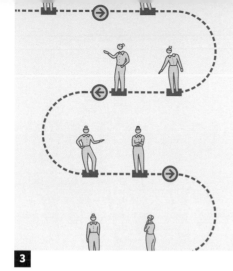

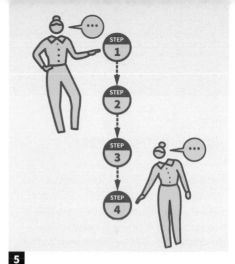

3

REINFORCE YOUR EXPECTATIONS

Follow through, routinely and positively insisting on your expectations being met every lesson or whenever they apply. If you weaken your commitment to any of your own expectations, this undermines their value and students' expectations will drop. Use **Positive Framing** to restate your expectations whenever necessary.

4

REDIRECT, CORRECT OR CHALLENGE

When expectations are not met, use positive correction to redirect students so they change their immediate behaviour. If you have asked for silence, it must be truly silent. If you have asked children to sit arms folded with pens down, then insist that everyone does this before you proceed. If people are talking, make sure they have stopped before you try to talk or invite another student to talk. Be very precise and direct about this every time.

5

SUSTAIN YOUR EXPECTATIONS

It is much easier to sustain high expectations if they become the norm as part of a set of routines; a set of behaviours that you do every day, every lesson. Construct a set of routines for walking into a room, conducting a discussion and organising group work or a practical session and all your other regular activities so that students know exactly what to do. Routines need to be rehearsed multiple times before becoming literally routine.

Attempt | Develop | Adapt | Practise | Test

SECTIONS: WHY? | **WHAT?** | HOW?

40 **BEHAVIOUR & RELATIONSHIPS** | CURRICULUM PLANNING
EXPLAINING & MODELLING | QUESTIONING & FEEDBACK
PRACTICE & RETRIEVAL | MODE B TEACHING

SIGNAL, PAUSE, INSIST

This is one of the most important routines in teaching because it is one teachers will use several times a lesson. Too often teachers over-rely on their voices to talk over the noise of a chatting class in order to gain attention. This can be difficult and hard to sustain. It can also run counter to the ideal of creating calm learning environments to rely on raised voices. A simple *signal — pause — insist* routine, allows teachers to move from one lesson phase to another calmly and efficiently. Everyone talking → Signal, pause, insist → Everyone listening. The more precise and consistent you are in giving the signal and insisting on the response, the more embedded the routine becomes.

1

CHOOSE A SIGNAL

Select a clear and easily reproduced signal that you will use to indicate that you want to regain full attention from the whole class. This might be: a raised hand; *3-2-1 and listening*; two sharp claps; using a small bell. It doesn't matter what you use as along as it can be used freely and repeatedly.

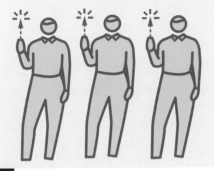

2

REHEARSE THE SIGNAL

Introduce the signal to each class in the establishment phase soon after meeting them. Practise the process of stopping and starting an activity using the signal so that it is clear what the signal is and what you want them to do on hearing it. This is likely to include facing you as the speaker and listening without talking in readiness for further instruction or questioning.

3

GIVE THE SIGNAL

During a lesson when you want to move from student activity to teacher input, stop what you are doing and give the agreed signal. Stand facing the class, scanning the room to make eye contact with everyone.

4

PAUSE

This is the crucial part. You must give students a short moment to adjust from being involved in working individually or talking to a partner to focusing on you. It's not instantaneous and you need to wait without speaking to allow this transition to happen naturally. Hold eye contact all the time. It's a mistake to give the signal and immediately begin to give further instructions because students will not be ready to hear them yet. When students are ready, you can affirm their positive response with a simple *"thank you"*.

5

INSIST

Before moving on you must be sure that everyone has given you the agreed response to the signal. If you allow even one student to continue talking while you begin to speak, you undermine the strength of the routine. If you can't get a 100% response through body language and eye contact, scanning the room in all the corners, front and back, low level reminders such as *"when we're ready, thank you"* or *"John, I need you listening, thank you"* can do the job. However, you might need a more strict response.

Attempt | Develop | Adapt | Practise | Test

SECTIONS: WHY? | **WHAT?** | HOW?

42 | **BEHAVIOUR & RELATIONSHIPS** | CURRICULUM PLANNING
EXPLAINING & MODELLING | QUESTIONING & FEEDBACK
PRACTICE & RETRIEVAL | MODE B TEACHING

POSITIVE FRAMING

This is a technique for establishing and maintaining high expectations through the use of positive reinforcement, encouragement and affirmative language. Instead of negative moaning or challenges that might be interpreted as personal criticism or arbitrary and unjust, teachers frame corrective directions through a positive frame. This works as a one-off strategy or, better still, as a complete approach.

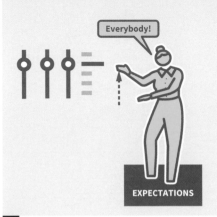

1

ESTABLISH YOUR EXPECTATIONS

In order for **Positive Framing** to work, it's important to have gone through the process of establishing expectations first. Students need to know what the expectations are so that they can then be re-affirmed through the framing technique.

2

AFFIRM POSITIVE RESPONSES FIRST

When dealing with a response to an instruction or running through a routine, give positive affirmation to students who meet the expectations before dealing with any who don't. *"Well done to this table; you're listening and ready to learn". "Thanks for an excellent response packing up the equipment from this group and this group". "So many excellent homework responses today. Well done people!"* This reinforces the message about the behaviours you want at the same time as acknowledging those who've responded appropriately. It keeps things in perspective.

REINFORCEMENT

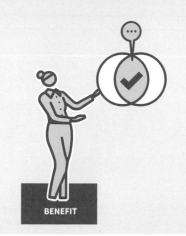

BENEFIT

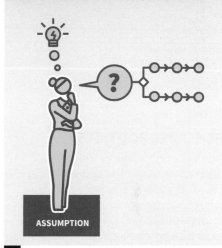

ASSUMPTION

3

FRAME CORRECTION AS POSITIVE REINFORCEMENT

When students do not meet your expectations, frame your response by reasserting what you want, not describing their behaviour. Instead of "*Sean and Mo, stop talking and turn around*" you say "*Sean, Mo… I'd like you both looking this way and listening thanks*". Instead of "*Michelle, you're late again and it's unacceptable to be so disorganised*" you say "*Michelle, I need you on time with all of your equipment.*" Nearly all corrective statements can be framed positively.

4

GIVE THE BENEFIT OF THE DOUBT

Instead of engaging with accusations and denials, assume students' best intentions and emphasise what you want to happen.

Teacher: *Louise, I need you focused on the task now. Thank you.*

Louise: *But I wasn't talking or disturbing anyone.*

Teacher: *OK, maybe you weren't but I need you focused and working hard now. Thank you.*

This can apply to talking or any other off-task behaviour. Bill Rogers calls this 'partial agreement'. "*Maybe that's true but….*"

5

ASSUME CONFUSION OVER DEFIANCE

Another form of positive framing is to feign confusion instead of issuing a challenge.

"*I wonder if this group did not quite hear the instructions?*"

"*There seems to be some confusion about our expectations here — can we just check we've all understood the routine?*"

This is transparent to all concerned but it keeps corrective language light, friendly and non-confrontational but also firm and definite about what is expected.

SECTIONS: WHY? | **WHAT?** | HOW?

44 **BEHAVIOUR & RELATIONSHIPS** | CURRICULUM PLANNING
EXPLAINING & MODELLING | QUESTIONING & FEEDBACK
PRACTICE & RETRIEVAL | MODE B TEACHING

REHEARSE ROUTINES

Routines are the bedrock of a positive behaviour management system. If everyone knows what to do, where to go, what to bring, how to respond and what happens in various situations, then it allows the focus to be on learning because the rest happens more or less automatically, with minimum fuss. Many aspects of school life happen the same every day, every lesson and lend themselves to being supported by clear routines. The key is to establish them and rehearse them so that they are known, understood and enacted consistently.

DESIGN

1

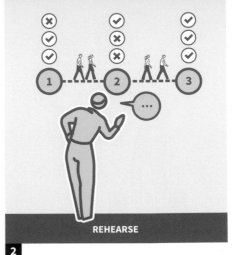

REHEARSE

2

DESIGN YOUR ROUTINES

Work out what you want students to do in every common situation they encounter. This might include arriving to class, entering and getting equipment ready, moving from a teacher-led phase to a groupwork phase, setting up and packing away practical equipment, recording homework, ending a lesson. Describe each routine in as few steps as possible.

WALK THROUGH EACH ROUTINE

The first time you introduce a routine, teach it explicitly and walk through it. Treat it like a rehearsal where you review the performance and then repeat it with improvements until you get the level of success you want to establish. Remember to **Establish your Expectations**. If you do not establish a high standard early on, it will be harder to address later.

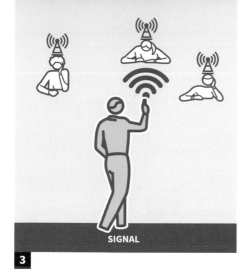

SIGNAL

3

MAKE ROUTINE

4

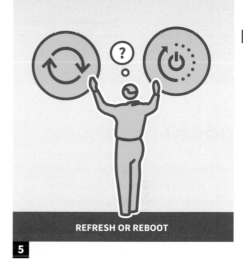

REFRESH OR REBOOT

5

TEACH THE SIGNALS

In the same way used in **Signal, Pause, Insist,** it is important for students to know when to enact a given routine. Some might be automatic — such as the routine for arriving at class. Some might need to be signalled by the teacher, such as the routine for packing away equipment. When a signal is needed, teach the signal, test it and reinforce it consistently.

MAKE ROUTINES ROUTINE

It is important to stick to the details of a routine so that they become automatic and do not require much reinforcement. This can feel artificial initially but it is worth persisting with routines so that they become the norm; the habits of everyday life that make boundaries clear and allow learning to be the focus of activity. If you allow routines to slip, then they cease to deliver the level of expectations you want and students lose a sense of what is really expected and acceptable.

REFRESH OR REBOOT

As far as possible, reinforce the routines, using **Positive Framing** and **Choices & Consequences** as regularly as needed. However, it's normal to experience some enforcement fatigue around any routines. When this happens teachers should take time to reboot the routine, re-setting the expectations, running through some explicit rehearsal so students reconnect with what they are meant to do in any given scenario. This can be a better option than issuing consequences to multiple students. If a routine has lapsed, reboot it.

Attempt | Develop | Adapt | Practise | Test

SECTIONS: WHY? | **WHAT?** | HOW?

46 | **BEHAVIOUR & RELATIONSHIPS** | CURRICULUM PLANNING
EXPLAINING & MODELLING | QUESTIONING & FEEDBACK
PRACTICE & RETRIEVAL | MODE B TEACHING

CHOICES & CONSEQUENCES

As part of the behaviour management system and routines in most settings, there will be a set of rules and agreed consequences for various levels of inappropriate behaviour. However, regardless of how strict or relatively relaxed a behaviour system might be, the teacher in the classroom has to use the system effectively to secure excellent behaviour. This can be done well when the emphasis is placed on students making the right choices in full knowledge of the consequences of the choices they make.

ESTABLISH THE RANGE

1

ESTABLISH THE RANGE OF FORMAL CONSEQUENCES

It's important for all students to know exactly what the range of consequence is. Make sure it is clear when any warnings will be given and the range of behaviours for which detentions or other consequences will be set. The consequences for very serious misdemeanours must be crystal clear. It can be useful to have a document or poster to refer to where the details are set out, in case of any confusion.

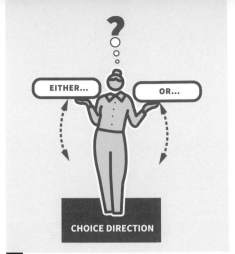

CHOICE DIRECTION

2

USE ASSERTIVE CHOICE DIRECTION

The principle is that if students choose to misbehave, they choose to receive the consequence. In some schools, sanctions are issued automatically; in others there is a warning step allowing reinforcement through the language of choice direction.

- *"James, you can either face forwards, concentrating on your work, or do a detention."*
- *"Amira, please follow the safety rules exactly, or you will sit at the desk and receive a phone call home."*

NARRATE CONSEQUENCES

CERTAINTY RULES

FAIRNESS ABOVE ALL

3

NARRATE THE CONSEQUENCES

When setting a consequence, explain why. This helps to make it clear to the student concerned whilst also reinforcing expectations for everyone else.

- *"Rachel, you've continued to talk after the warning, which disrupts our learning, so you now have a detention after school. "*
- *"Sadiq, you have arrived late to class so that is an automatic demerit as you know."*
- *"Sam, you have forgotten your kit twice, so that means a lunchtime detention tomorrow."*

4

MAINTAIN THE PRINCIPLE OF CERTAINTY OVER SEVERITY

An important aspect of a consequences system is that students must all believe that the teacher will definitely follow through; that certain behaviours will definitely lead to consequences; that detentions or other consequences issued, will happen; that you mean what you say. The severity of a consequence is less critical. If consequences issued do not happen, it undermines you and makes it harder to manage later.

5

USE CONSEQUENCES JUDICIOUSLY

Fairness is important in any system so it is important to be as consistent as possible when giving consequences for certain behaviours. If you use consequences too infrequently or inconsistently, it undermines you. If you give out consequences too liberally, without narration or reinforcing routines, it can create a negative culture that also undermines you. Give students the chance to make good choices; support them to make this a habit.

Attempt | Develop | Adapt | Practise | Test

WALKTHRU SERIES

CURRICULUM PLANNING

01
BEHAVIOUR &
RELATIONSHIPS
PAGE 34

02

03
EXPLAINING &
MODELLING
PAGE 66

04
QUESTIONING &
FEEDBACK
PAGE 88

05
PRACTICE &
RETRIEVAL
PAGE 110

06
MODE B
TEACHING
PAGE 132

There is an important interplay between curriculum and pedagogy: what we teach and how we teach it. This set of WalkThrus explores a range of levels of thinking about curriculum from the big picture overview down to the fine details of what students should know, the experiences we should provide and the kinds of questions we should ask. This is linked to concepts that we feel are important, helping teachers to design a curriculum that is coherent, rich in knowledge and experience and where attention is given to the hinterland as well as the core. Alongside the day-to-day classroom practice that features in most of our WalkThrus, this set is slightly more conceptual and will probably be most useful during a curriculum review process and in the planning stages of any new unit of work.

SECTIONS: WHY? | **WHAT?** | HOW?

50

BEHAVIOUR & RELATIONSHIPS | **CURRICULUM PLANNING**
EXPLAINING & MODELLING | QUESTIONING & FEEDBACK
PRACTICE & RETRIEVAL | MODE B TEACHING

DESIGNING A KNOWLEDGE–RICH CURRICULUM

The concept of a knowledge-rich curriculum has gained prominence in the UK in recent years. It's not a tightly defined concept but we believe that, viewed in the right spirit, it provides teachers with a useful lens through which to review and construct a curriculum. Embracing a breadth of knowledge in many forms, it's important for teachers to be deliberate in their planning of what students will learn in order to support them constructing rich, extensive schema for a range of knowledge domains.

Our definition of knowledge-rich is presented here.

WALKTHRUs IN THIS SERIES

CURRICULUM PLANNING

1

LET KNOWLEDGE DRIVE YOUR PHILOSOPHY

At the heart of this idea is the belief that knowledge is empowering, unlocking doors, providing a foundation for achieving success, reaching deep understanding and being creative. The more children know, the more they can learn. The challenge is to identify which areas of knowledge to focus on but it starts with the conviction that knowledge matters.

2

CONSIDER A BROAD RANGE OF KNOWLEDGE FORMS

For every subject or topic, think of all the knowledge you think is important, referencing expert sources where you need to:

- **Declarative:** What are the key facts that all children should know?
- **Procedural:** What are the things that all children should be able to do? (You might call these 'skills')
- **Experiential:** What knowledge can only be gained first-hand, by experiencing or doing certain activities?

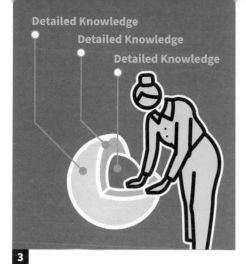

Detailed Knowledge

Detailed Knowledge

Detailed Knowledge

3

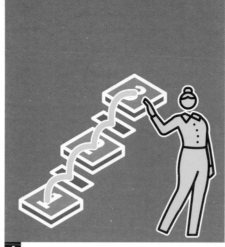

4

5

SPECIFY THE KNOWLEDGE IN DETAIL

Go through the knowledge areas you want to include and specify the exact core elements of what students should know in as much detail as is possible, appropriate for their stage of learning e.g.:

- What, exactly, should every child know about the Romans?
- What, exactly, would you expect them to know about *Of Mice and Men*?
- What, exactly, would you expect them to know about sound and light?

SEQUENCE AND MAP THE KNOWLEDGE COHERENTLY

Sequence the knowledge content in all its forms such that there is a coherent flow, allowing ideas to build on secure foundations, staged deliberately step by step building towards challenging goals. Map this out so that everyone involved in delivering the curriculum can see how the content is sequenced over time. Check that you are **Sequencing Concepts in Small Steps** and using **Coherent Mapping**.

TEACH KNOWLEDGE TO BE REMEMBERED, NOT MERELY ENCOUNTERED

Plan the sequencing of your curriculum so that elements of it are regularly returned to, supporting students to accumulate knowledge over time, feeding previous topics into current topics supported by **Practice and Retrieval** strategies.

SECTIONS: WHY? | **WHAT?** | HOW?

52

BEHAVIOUR & RELATIONSHIPS | **CURRICULUM PLANNING**
EXPLAINING & MODELLING | QUESTIONING & FEEDBACK
PRACTICE & RETRIEVAL | MODE B TEACHING

SEQUENCE CONCEPTS IN SMALL STEPS

In order to form secure schema, students need to assimilate new learning connecting it to what they already know. This is constrained by the extent of their prior knowledge and the inherent limitations of working memory: we can't deal with too many ideas at once. Many areas of learning are built around a logical set of ideas or steps that build on each other or follow a sequence. This could be the components of writing, mathematical operations, a dance, making food, understanding a historical event. The more confident and knowledgeable students are, the bigger these steps can be and vice versa.

WALKTHRUs IN THIS SERIES

CURRICULUM PLANNING

1

IDENTIFY PRE-REQUISITE KNOWLEDGE

Analyse the area of learning in hand and begin to consider how it could be broken down into a series of steps. Consider what your assumptions are about the prior knowledge students will need to have in order to engage with the new material. This could be conceptual, vocabulary-based or some level of physical competence. It will be necessary to check that students all have this knowledge before proceeding and to address the gaps where they exist.

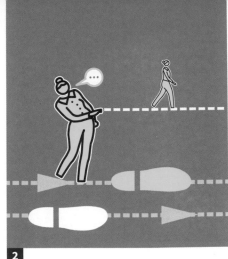

2

IDENTIFY THE MOST BASIC FIRST STEPS

This is often the most important decision: where to begin? If students are not confident with the first, most basic steps, then they are more likely to struggle thereafter. What are the first new ideas that you think students should have; the basics on which all the rest depends? This could be some vocabulary. It could be establishing a mental or spatial model for a phenomenon or mathematical operation. It could be the big picture stage in a composition process.

3

4

5

IDENTIFY THE SERIES OF NEXT STEPS

Build on the first steps, breaking down the concepts and skills further, looking for common misconceptions and the more difficult stages as well as the more straightforward steps. Once you have worked it out in principle, run through the steps to check that , if followed, students would end up having succeeded in understanding a concept or performed the task concerned to the level required.

DESIGN INSTRUCTIONAL INPUTS

For each of the steps, consider how you will introduce them to students. This could be by selecting **Explaining and Modelling** tools. It could by providing students with the necessary hands-on experience they need to gain the foundational experiential knowledge needed to understand the ideas in hand.

DESIGN PRACTICE TASKS

Very often, in order for students to succeed, they will need to practice each of the steps one by one and then in short sequences before attempting to practice the whole sequence. Select the appropriate **Practice and Retrieval** tools to support students in gaining the level of fluency they need before proceeding to introduce new steps.

SECTIONS: WHY? | **WHAT?** | HOW?

54

BEHAVIOUR & RELATIONSHIPS | **CURRICULUM PLANNING**
EXPLAINING & MODELLING | QUESTIONING & FEEDBACK
PRACTICE & RETRIEVAL | MODE B TEACHING

COHERENT MAPPING

A coherent curriculum is one where learning
experiences, knowledge and skills are
sequenced and woven together such that
students form a deep understanding both
within and between the various subjects or
knowledge domains. This requires vertical
planning, so that new knowledge builds
on secure foundations at every point as
students move through the curriculum. It
also requires horizontal planning so that
links between areas of concurrent learning
are made deliberately such that learning is
enriched and deepened.

1

IDENTIFY CORE CONCEPTS AND BIG QUESTIONS

Try to express your curriculum goals as a set
of big questions and set out the fundamental
concepts that underpin them. This might
include such things as particles, energy and
rate of change in science; chronology and
change and continuity in history.

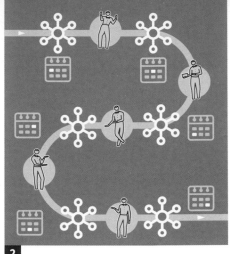

2

MAP THE BIG PICTURE

Scope out the main areas of learning
that will provide the overall structure of
knowledge to be covered in the year or unit
of learning. Organise units into a sequence
that makes sense in terms of conceptual
flow and hierarchy of core concepts and big
questions. This might be the broad science
topics; periods of history and key elements of
history's disciplinary knowledge; the range of
genres, composers and aspects of theory and
composition in music.

3

MAP THE SPIRALLING OF CONCEPTS

Scope out the opportunities to space concepts and themes spiralling vertically over time. Revisit topics at incremental levels of difficulty so that students can build their schema as they mature, making conceptual links and integrating prior knowledge with new learning each time a topic comes around again.

4

GO DEEPER

Once you have a solid spiralled big picture curriculum framework in mind, plan the next level of depth; the more specific content of each topic or unit. Check that each unit links to prior knowledge and builds towards units that lie ahead. Ensure that you **Pitch It Up** so that there is good level of challenge for all students. Be sure to **Blend Knowledge And Experience**.

5

MAKE AUTHENTIC CONNECTIONS

As your curriculum map takes shape, look to the maps in other areas to see where you can make connections that are allow knowledge areas to be mutually reinforcing and enriching. Don't force artificial links where none exist, highlight the authentic connections between subjects and concepts that arise.

Attempt | Develop | Adapt | Practise | Test

SECTIONS: WHY? | **WHAT?** | HOW?

56

BEHAVIOUR & RELATIONSHIPS | **CURRICULUM PLANNING**
EXPLAINING & MODELLING | QUESTIONING & FEEDBACK
PRACTICE & RETRIEVAL | MODE B TEACHING

BLEND KNOWLEDGE & EXPERIENCE

Some knowledge we acquire cannot be taught directly; it has to be developed through experience. This will include anything that requires physical skill — the knowledge of how it feels to perform a task can only be gained by doing it. It will include the experience of reading a poem aloud; taking measurements in a workshop or science lab; seeing artefacts in a museum or a play at a theatre; feeling the way the force of attraction between a pair of magnets varies with the distance between them. This kind of knowledge needs planning like any other.

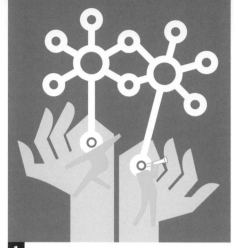

1

2

WALKTHRUs IN THIS SERIES

CURRICULUM PLANNING

EXAMINE LEARNING GOALS THROUGH THE LENS OF EXPERIENCES

Review the content of your curriculum to establish where students will need to have hands-on experiences in order to develop a secure schema for the knowledge in hand. Think about the assumptions you make about experiences they would ideally have had in order to fully engage with each aspect of the curriculum.

IDENTIFY WHERE EXPERIENTIAL LEARNING HAS INTRINSIC VALUE

What hands-on experiences are part of the curriculum on their own terms? This could be aspects of performance and oracy, visits to specific places, practical activities in science or technology where the experience of performing the task is a learning goal in itself.

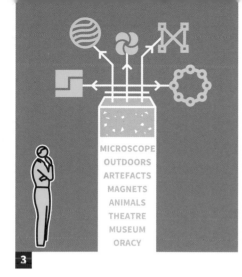

MICROSCOPE
OUTDOORS
ARTEFACTS
MAGNETS
ANIMALS
THEATRE
MUSEUM
ORACY

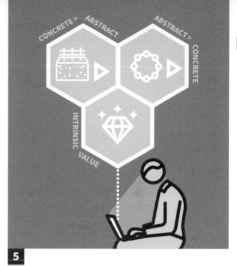

3

4

5

IDENTIFY WHERE CONCRETE EXPERIENCE IS THE FOUNDATION FOR ABSTRACT IDEAS

Highlight areas where hands-on experience is a pre-requisite for deeper conceptual understanding. This might include using manipulatives such as Cuisenaire rods in maths; making a motor in the study of electromagnetism; handling artefacts or materials or living things in order to appreciate their physical properties; experiencing certain environments before analysing their features.

IDENTIFY WHERE CONCEPTUAL UNDERSTANDING IS PREREQUISITE

Establish where it might be better for students to acquire a level of foundational knowledge prior to engaging in experiential learning. This might include learning the terminology and underlying model for a science experiment before attempting it; studying a play before seeing a live performance of it; establishing the key narrative of a historical event before a museum or site visit.

MAP THE EXPERIENTIAL ELEMENTS INTO THE WIDER FRAMEWORK

With these three categories of experiential learning in mind, map them into your wider curriculum plan in the appropriate place, writing them into schemes of learning, ensuring they become entitlements for all students, not optional extras.

SECTIONS: WHY? | **WHAT?** | HOW?

58

BEHAVIOUR & RELATIONSHIPS | **CURRICULUM PLANNING**
EXPLAINING & MODELLING | QUESTIONING & FEEDBACK
PRACTICE & RETRIEVAL | MODE B TEACHING

PITCH IT UP

Alongside expectations of behaviour, high expectations of the standards students should reach are vital. If you don't expect students to reach a certain standard, they probably won't. To make sure we have the highest expectations appropriate for our students, it helps to **Pitch it Up**. This entails exploring all the possible opportunities for taking a more challenging path, eliminating low level tasks that don't push students forward with enough intensity. Balancing this with the need for practice and consolidation can be a challenge but it should be part of the curriculum design process.

1

AIM FOR DEPTH BEFORE SPEED

Learning is not a race. Getting to the end more quickly can lead to more shallow learning. Depth means:

- Giving students a wider range of problems to explore within a topic
- Aiming for deeper levels of analysis or sophistication in writing or providing explanations
- Applying knowledge to unfamiliar scenarios to test depth of understanding

Speed can be useful — in terms of developing fluency or, for example, jumping over more simple ideas in maths to reach higher level material sooner. But aim for depth first.

2

EXPECT SOPHISTICATION, ACCURACY AND PRECISION

Set a higher bar for expected standards. Insist that students produce a higher level of accuracy and precision in their work appropriate for their age or stage. This could mean: insisting on using the correct formal terminology, expressing ideas in a more focused logical manner; using more appropriate formal speech codes; drawing graphs and diagrams with more precision, saying words in French with a more authentic accent. It means, not accepting sub-standard versions of responses when a more accurate version is within reach.

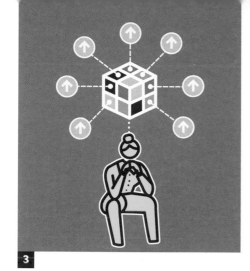

SELECT THE MORE DEMANDING CURRICULUM OPTIONS

When choosing texts, reading extracts, case studies, examples of compositions — there will be a range in terms of the level of challenge and accessibility. If you **Pitch it Up**, you go for a more challenging option instead of a more accessible one. Students do not learn to read difficult texts if they don't get the chance. This needs to form part of an overall plan, building confidence leading towards ambitious goals. But, at any point, consider whether a more demanding option would be within reach. If so, make that choice.

ELIMINATE MEDIOCRITY — e.g. LOW-LEVEL TASKS

Review your lessons from the perspective of 'thinking'. Do your tasks require students to think hard about the meaning of the concepts; do they need to engage in generative recall of foundational knowledge, consciously making connections with prior knowledge to solve problems? Can tasks be easily done without much recall or cognitive processing? e.g. Is that grid-fill, wordsearch or poster activity possible without really remembering or understanding much? If so, ditch them or change them.

INCREASE THE INTENSITY

Consider whether deeper levels of learning would be achieved by increasing the intensity of the processes in hand. Is there enough drive and sense of purpose? This might be about the rate of completion of questions; the level of focus and intensity in carrying out a practical task; the number of repetitions in a practice routine with knowledge retrieval or the practice on an instrument. Increasing the work rate in any task can be an important factor in deepening learning; not making practice more difficult but making it more intense.

Attempt | Develop | Adapt | Practise | Test

SECTIONS: WHY? | **WHAT?** | HOW?

60

BEHAVIOUR & RELATIONSHIPS | **CURRICULUM PLANNING**
EXPLAINING & MODELLING | QUESTIONING & FEEDBACK
PRACTICE & RETRIEVAL | MODE B TEACHING

PLAN FOR READING

It is well understood that improving students' reading confidence is central to the curriculum as a whole. Teachers across most subjects and phases have a role to play through their curriculum planning. Planning for literacy includes teachers examining how students' fluency in reading and their knowledge of the subject can be mutually reinforcing. It has implications for selecting appropriate reading material and designing activities so that reading is embedded in the routines of lessons.

1

MAKE READING CENTRAL TO YOUR PLANNING

Rather than planning reading as an after-thought, where having planned your curriculum you shoe-horn reading activities in, try to integrate reading from the beginning. For example, in science, make developing students' capacity to read scientific texts part of your curriculum thinking alongside the science concepts themselves. At every stage possible, locate opportunities for students to learn about the topics you cover through reading about them.

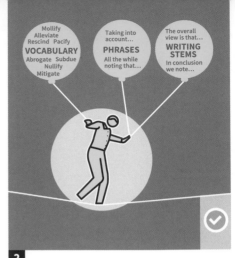

2

IDENTIFY KEY VOCABULARY, PHRASES AND WRITING STEMS

Teach all the words and phrases needed to understand a text as explicitly as possible. For any given topic, generate a list of key words and phrases, creating resources setting them out. It is easier to engage in conscious rehearsal with vocabulary and elements of writing if they are made explicit. Include common writing stems for opening paragraphs and phrases for linking ideas. Focus on a tight list that students can practise rather than a comprehensive list that is overwhelming.

3

PLAN READING RESOURCES

Make it an embedded component in your planning of schemes of learning that you select texts for students to read about the topic in hand, setting aside the time to do the reading in lessons. Where possible link the text to the vocabulary/phrase lists so that students encounter the words and phrases in context. Pitch the level of reading so that it provides a good balance of challenge and accessibility, focusing on the knowledge content of the subject curriculum.

4

PLAN COMPREHENSION ACTIVITIES

In addition to developing students' capacity to decode and say the words they encounter with confidence, they also need to read for meaning which requires them to engage in comprehension activities. These can include: answering comprehension questions based on the text; summarising key points or re-phrasing in their own words verbally or in writing; applying the content to problem-solving activities; or following written instructions.

5

BUILD TOWARDS INDEPENDENT READING

Make it explicit that students' goal is to be able to read relevant texts independently as part of their overall learning journey. Build towards this by designing reading routines involving tasks to be completed as part of students' study time linked to checking processes that explore how well they have understood the material. This could include retrieval practice, comprehension tasks or structured discussions based on set reading.

SECTIONS: WHY? | **WHAT?** | HOW?

62

BEHAVIOUR & RELATIONSHIPS | **CURRICULUM PLANNING**
EXPLAINING & MODELLING | QUESTIONING & FEEDBACK
PRACTICE & RETRIEVAL | MODE B TEACHING

TIERED QUESTIONS & PROBLEMS

An ever-present challenge with teaching is that students progress at different rates. We have common challenging goals in mind for all students but they will not all progress towards them in the same way. The challenge is to set students appropriate levels of practice without lowering longer-term expectations. Telling students they 'only need to learn some of the material' puts a ceiling on their achievement. By tiering challenges and problems sets, all students can progress through the steps in different ways whilst keeping longer term goals in mind.

WALKTHRUs IN THIS SERIES

CURRICULUM PLANNING

1

MAP THE STAGES OF DIFFICULTY IN A TOPIC

As part of your **Coherent Mapping** process within a topic, identify the stages in the hierarchy of difficulty as students progress through it. This could be expressed in terms of depth of knowledge or level of proficiency; it could be expressed in terms of the specific question-types that they should be able to answer; it could be useful to reference exemplar material to illustrate the stages.

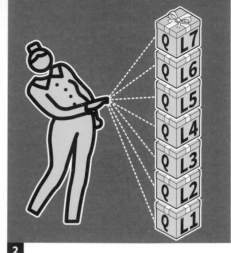

2

ASSEMBLE QUESTIONS TO SUPPORT PRACTICE AT EACH LEVEL OF DIFFICULTY

Gather or produce questions or tasks that provide practice in a very specific aspect of the curriculum. In order to develop fluency, students will need to have repeated opportunities to succeed at each level before moving on. Make sure you have enough practice questions and tasks to support the least confident students to continue their practice.

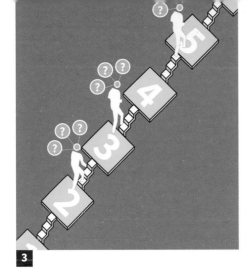

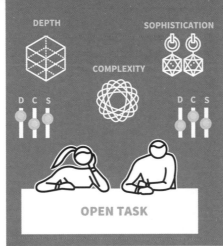

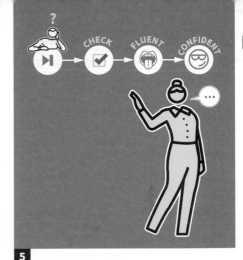

3

PRODUCE TIERED QUESTION SETS THAT STEP UP THROUGH THE LEVELS

Compile sets of questions that take several questions from each of the tiered banks, starting with the easiest, moving up to the most difficult. Include enough questions at each level so that students can practise within a level for longer than others if needed. Make the hardest questions a genuine stretch for your highest attaining students so that there is no risk of them being under-challenged or finishing prematurely.

4

DESIGN OPEN TASKS THAT ALLOW RESPONSES AT A RANGE OF LEVELS

In some subject contexts it will be more useful to design tasks that allow students to produce responses to varying levels of depth, complexity and sophistication with the same stimulus material and instructions. Here it will be important to **Set the Standards** supported by exemplar material, so that students do not under pitch their output relative to their capability. Make certain that every student can achieve within the task and that every student will be challenged by it.

5

DESIGN 'WHAT NEXT' ROUTINES

With tiered questions or open tasks, rehearse the routines students should follow when they are ready to move up to the next level of difficulty. This might include checking answers, demonstrating their fluency and confidence to you before having permission to move on; it might be a self-directed review of work against the agreed success criteria. Ideally your routines will mean that students are never waiting having finished or having got stuck; they will know what to do next.

SECTIONS: WHY? | **WHAT?** | HOW?

64

BEHAVIOUR & RELATIONSHIPS | **CURRICULUM PLANNING**
EXPLAINING & MODELLING | QUESTIONING & FEEDBACK
PRACTICE & RETRIEVAL | MODE B TEACHING

DELIVER CORE; SIGNPOST HINTERLAND

A central challenge in curriculum design is that there is just too much to fit in! We have to make choices: what is core and must be taught and what, therefore, do we have to leave out or make only passing reference to? Christine Counsell promotes the idea that teachers view this in terms of the concept of 'hinterland'. Beyond the core material that we cover lies the hinterland. This is important because it provides the background against which the core content exists offering a range of perspectives and connecting ideas. The idea is not to forget it — but to signpost it explicitly.

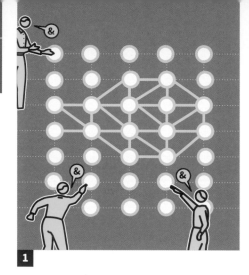

1

ESTABLISH THE CORE

Go through the mapping exercise described in **Coherent Mapping**. It's important that the selection of curriculum content is coherent with concepts that build on each other and span the range of ideas in the subject. However, as you do this, be conscious of the alternative choices you might have made. Which literary texts, case-studies, places, artists, historical figures and events, areas of science or musical genres are not in the core but remain highly significant to the subject overall?

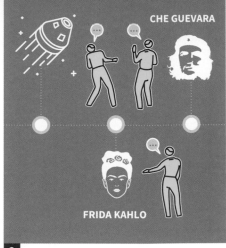

2

MAP OUT THE HINTERLAND IN BROAD TERMS

Survey the range of curriculum elements you decided not to include and prioritise within that list the areas that might play a supporting role to the core. Keep it as general as you can to allow for a responsive approach. This might include literary genres from which you have chosen specific texts; areas of science (such as astronomy and cosmology) that you only have time to dip into; the life histories of key figures who feature in your core curriculum; whole periods of history you can't deliver directly.

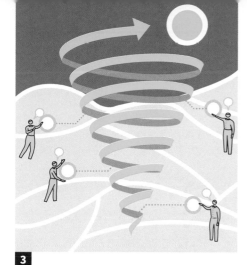

3

PLAN HINTERLAND REFERENCES AS CONTEXT FOR THE CORE

Make explicit links during instructional inputs or via the selection of reading materials, between the hinterland areas you've highlighted and the core spiralled curriculum. This might include historical contexts to the texts you study in literature; historical events happening in other countries in parallel to those you are studying; similar climate change events in other countries to those you are studying but that you don't have time to include; the life story of a scientist that adds context to her discoveries and ideas.

4

ENGAGE STUDENTS IN HINTERLAND RESEARCH TASKS

Provide students with structured research tasks that require them to find out about areas of the related curriculum beyond the core. They could provide additional case study examples about geographical features or cities, poems they find interesting, historical events in other countries using an idea called 'Meanwhile elsewhere', life stories of scientists, examples of artists, authors and musicians and their work within or across genres. Sharing these as a class can bring the richness of the hinterland into play

5

ADOPT A RESPONSIVE ORGANIC APPROACH

Perhaps more than any other strategy — adopt a mindset that it is always worthwhile adding depth to the learning by telling stories, responding to events and sharing ideas as they come up — even if they are not directly covered in the curriculum. This could be a news story, the history behind a scientific discovery, a passage from another Dickens novel to contrast with the one you are reading or the story of Dickens as a person. A rich range of hinterland references tell students that all this is out there to learn about, adding curricular texture and depth to the current core focus or to explore in the future.

Attempt | Develop | Adapt | Practise | Test

EXPLAINING & MODELLING

A central feature of effective teaching is the process of enabling students to develop their knowledge and understanding of concepts and processes and the ability to apply their learning to a range of situations. Explaining and modelling are vital elements of any teacher's repertoire of techniques. Drawing on the evidence base described in the Why section including ideas from Willingham, Wiliam, Berger and Shimamura, these WalkThrus cover several key aspects of effective teachers' practice from building their vocabulary, exploring difficult concepts and producing sophisticated pieces of work at a high standard.

SECTIONS: WHY? | **WHAT?** | HOW?

68

BEHAVIOUR & RELATIONSHIPS | CURRICULUM PLANNING
EXPLAINING & MODELLING | QUESTIONING & FEEDBACK
PRACTICE & RETRIEVAL | MODE B TEACHING

WORKED EXAMPLES & BACKWARD FADING

One of the ideas that comes from Cognitive Load Theory is that novices learn more successfully from studying a series of complete worked examples of problems or tasks than they do if asked to problem-solve independently. This is because the cognitive load is reduced if we learn the overall method separately from trying to apply it to a particular question. Once we know the method, it is easier to apply it successfully. Teachers should make sure they're providing enough worked examples. The backward fading technique provides a good model for moving from guided to independent practice through worked examples.

WALKTHRUs IN THIS SERIES

EXPLAINING & MODELLING

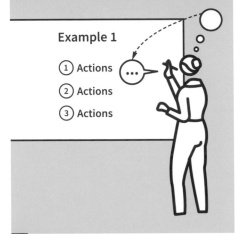

1 **EXAMPLE 1**

FULLY WORKED TO INTRODUCE THE METHOD OR IDEAS

Introduce the first example of a question that you are aiming for students to answer. With their attention secured, go through the problem on the board, producing a model answer, talking through what you are doing as you write. It is often better to model it live than to produce a pre-prepared example. With the answer in view, talk through each of your steps again and check for student understanding of each one. *"What did I do here?". "Why did I choose to write that phrase?"*

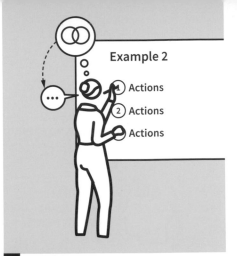

2 **EXAMPLE 2**

FULLY WORKED FOR REINFORCEMENT

Repeat the process with another example, taking care to draw out the ways in which it is similar to the first example and the ways it is different. The similarities should serve to reinforce the general idea or method you are teaching. The differences should illustrate how the method works with different cases (numbers, words, phrases, examples). Again, be sure to narrate your thinking and then to check for understanding. *"How is this example the same/different to the previous example?"*

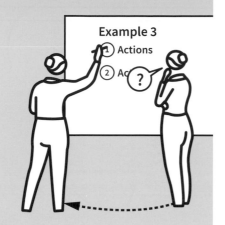

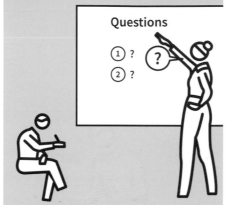

3 EXAMPLE 3

PARTIALLY WORKED FOR STUDENTS TO FINISH OFF

This time, introduce a question and begin to answer it, perhaps doing the first couple of lines of a maths problem or providing some of the ideas in a written response, following the pattern or procedure you introduced in the first two examples. Give students time to complete the question and then check for answers, errors and any variations or misunderstanding.

4 EXAMPLE 4

CUED START FOR STUDENT COMPLETION

Students should now be ready for a practice phase. Initially, set one or more questions, of the same type as the examples, giving information so that they are cued i.e. where you have started them off or signalled the way to begin.

5 EXAMPLE 5

COMPLETED INDEPENDENTLY

When ready, set one or more questions of the same type that you have modelled where students have to undertake the whole thinking process independently. Stress the need to follow the details of the modelled examples. Follow-up with self-assessment, checking for accuracy including process questions to verify that the methods are understood as well as being copied. You may need to include a range of questions of varying difficulty in order for independent completion to be successful and challenging for all learners.

Attempt | Develop | Adapt | Practise | Test

SECTIONS: WHY? | **WHAT?** | HOW?

70

BEHAVIOUR & RELATIONSHIPS | CURRICULUM PLANNING
EXPLAINING & MODELLING | QUESTIONING & FEEDBACK
PRACTICE & RETRIEVAL | MODE B TEACHING

DUAL CODING:
RECOUNT & RECALL

Paivio's Dual Coding Theory was concerned only with the recall of lists of cognitively unchallenging material. Later psychologists developed his work to cover understanding of more complex content.

Recount and Recall allows teachers to share their schema with students visually as well as with words. The incorporation of embodied cognition by students — drawing and tracing — bypasses many constraints of working memory. Understanding is strengthened through peer explanation and this provides a superb opportunity for oral rehearsal in preparation for later writing.

1

CONSTRUCT & EXPLAIN YOUR DIAGRAM

Start by saying that the diagram you are about to build on the whiteboard, is a model of your schema. Explain that you are aiming for each student to have the same schema in their head by the end of the process. Emphasise that you are keen for each student to understand the topic as well as you — the expert — does.

You can do this through live drawing with a visualiser, or through the gradual display with a prepared slide presentation.

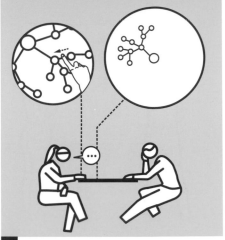

2

COPY & EXPLAIN THE BRANCH WITH TRACING OF THE LINES

After explaining the organisation and meaning of the first part of the diagram, direct students to explain it back to their partner. While doing so, the students trace the line related to the area being summarised. Student listeners also trace the corresponding line on their diagram. When complete, switch roles.

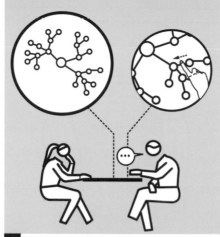

3

REPEAT THE SAME PROCESS UNTIL THE WHOLE DIAGRAM IS COMPLETE

Continue to work in this way until the whole diagram has been copied, then summarised to a partner and every line traced. To ensure students aren't merely reading the words copied, establish a rule that every keyword needs to be explained in, say, three sentences. This will ensure students articulate their thoughts. Listening partners can also ask questions related to details and, also, to any potential cross–diagram connection.

4

RECOUNT THE WHOLE DIAGRAM TO PARTNER, WITH TRACING

If time allows, give students an opportunity to explain the whole map — in the same fashion — to their partner. And repeat roles when the first is finished.

5

REDRAW THE WHOLE DIAGRAM FROM MEMORY

Finally, remove the diagrams from sight. To start, ask the students to play back their explanations silently in their head at the same time as tracing the diagram with their index finger. Once they realise they have a solid memory, direct them to pick up their pens and redraw the diagram from memory. When complete, ask them to compare their diagram with their original and search out any gaps or inaccuracies. Stress that they can apply this technique to any topic.

Attempt | Develop | Adapt | **Practise** | Test

SECTIONS: WHY? | **WHAT?** | HOW?

72 BEHAVIOUR & RELATIONSHIPS | CURRICULUM PLANNING
EXPLAINING & MODELLING | QUESTIONING & FEEDBACK
PRACTICE & RETRIEVAL | MODE B TEACHING

DELIBERATE VOCABULARY DEVELOPMENT

In order for students to become fluent in the use of complex subject-specific terminology and more general vocabulary, the process of learning new words needs to be considered deliberately and explicitly as part of teacher instruction. Students with the weakest prior knowledge and most limited vocabulary will find this more difficult; new words do not just 'sink in' and, in the absence of deliberate practice, new words are likely to be forgotten all too easily. These steps support a deliberate vocabulary development process for all learners.

1

SPECIFY AND DEFINE THE WORDS

Compile lists or a glossary of words that you know students will need to know or highlight them in the texts and resources they will use. Provide definitions for these words so that students can explain them in terms they know. As and when new words crop up, make sure that they too are defined. It's not possible to learn terminology that has no meaning in terms students already understand.

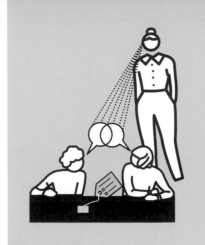

2

SAY THE WORDS

Make sure that all students say all the words they need to learn. This can be done in various ways:

- **Chorally:** All students repeat the words in call and response style. This is useful when modelling pronunciation.
- **In pairs:** Engineer structured paired discussions or question and answer exchanges so that students need to use the words they are learning. Circulate to check for accuracy.
- **Rapid fire:** Check that individual students can use the words through individual questioning or call and response.

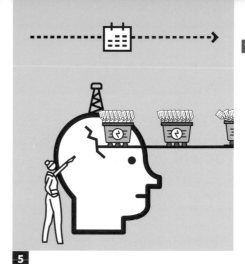

READ WORDS IN CONTEXT

Wherever possible, ensure that the target vocabulary is encountered embedded in texts that students will read. This give the words a context that supports understanding and recall. It can help to pre-learn words prior to reading a text. Alternatively it can be important to interrupt reading when new words arise to ensure that they are explored for meaning in that context.

PRACTISE USING THE WORDS VERBALLY AND IN WRITING

Students must practice using words for them to form part of the repertoire of words they can actually use. Give students practice tasks that require the words to be used in writing and in structured discussions. Reinforce the expectation that students use the new terminology whenever relevant, rather than reverting to more familiar basic terms.

ENGAGE IN WORD-BASED RETRIEVAL PRACTICE

Use glossaries and **Knowledge Organisers** to support regular retrieval practice using the target vocabulary. Students must be required to recall the words from memory — not relying on looking them up. At first this may require some high intensity initial practise followed by weekly and monthly reviews later on. Test that students know what words mean, can identity their correct use in context and can use them in speech and in writing themselves.

Attempt | Develop | Adapt | Practise | Test

SECTIONS: WHY? | **WHAT?** | HOW?

74

BEHAVIOUR & RELATIONSHIPS | CURRICULUM PLANNING
EXPLAINING & MODELLING | QUESTIONING & FEEDBACK
PRACTICE & RETRIEVAL | MODE B TEACHING

BIG PICTURE, SMALL PICTURE — ZOOM IN, ZOOM OUT

As described by Shimamura in his MARGE model, it can help students to form coherent schema if teachers front-load the process of organising information in the way ideas are introduced. This is the R of MARGE: Relate. One aspect of this is to illustrate how ideas are connected; that specific ideas form part of a bigger picture and that we can arrange concepts in categories or at various levels of depth and generalisation. We can then compare and contrast related ideas in order to deepen our understanding of the topic in hand.

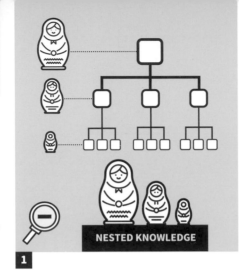

NESTED KNOWLEDGE

1

SET OUT THE BIG PICTURE

Present a broad overview of a topic. Highlight the sub-divisions; the range of sub-categories in a wider category. This could be:

- Something physical, like organ systems: Circulatory/Digestive/Nervous/Muscular-skeletal.
- Categories of energy sources: fossil fuels/renewable and non-renewable.
- A timeline: Overview of Nazi Germany '21-'45: Rise of Hitler to WWII. We get a feel for the sequence of events before studying each one in depth.

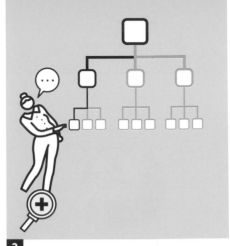

2

ZOOM IN — ORIENTATE!

Focus on a specific element but make the connection to the **Big Picture** very explicit.

- A cell in the body is always part of a bigger organ system.
- A specific example of a fossil fuel fits in a wider category.
- A historical event is part of a wider frame: WWII '39-'45 | Events in '44 | D-Day Landings.

The aim is for students to see where the knowledge in hand belongs in relation to other knowledge.

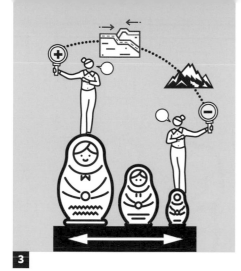

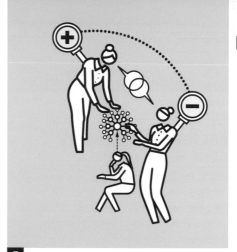

3

ZOOM IN AND ZOOM OUT STEP BY STEP

Whether you start big or small, continually make the link to and from details of knowledge to a bigger frame and back again.

- Kathmandu earthquake case-study | earthquakes | hazards/tectonic activity
- "Full of scorpions is my mind" | Macbeth's guilt | Macbeth's character | complex Shakespearean 'heroes'?
- Regular pentagon | Pentagons |Family of Polygons ←→ Shapes.

4

REHEARSE AND CHECK FOR UNDERSTANDING

Explore the links explicitly yourself but then make sure that students can make the links themselves. Follow through with **Check for Understanding** routines. Engage students in **Think Pair Share** or **Elaborative Interrogation** so that they can make the zoom in / zoom out connections independently.

5

USE THE ZOOM IN/ZOOM OUT PROCESS ROUTINELY

Establish the routine that, in any learning process, you consciously, explicitly look at layers of detail within a wider frame. This helps to organise information to form sound schema, to make connections as new knowledge is encountered and it helps with retrieval later on. Use resources like number lines and timelines as visual displays so that you can refer to them easily and repeatedly.

Attempt | Develop | Adapt | Practise | Test

SECTIONS: WHY? | **WHAT?** | HOW?

76 BEHAVIOUR & RELATIONSHIPS | CURRICULUM PLANNING
EXPLAINING & MODELLING | QUESTIONING & FEEDBACK
PRACTICE & RETRIEVAL | MODE B TEACHING

ABSTRACT MODELS WITH CONCRETE EXAMPLES

One of the biggest challenges students face is the need to make a connection between concrete examples and abstract conceptualisations. This might be understanding how words behave grammatically; how material properties relate to their particle structures; how general mathematical ideas relate to specific problems; how simplified diagrams relate to the complex real world. Teachers can help through linking examples and models deliberately and explicitly.

1

DEMONSTRATE AN EXAMPLE

Introduce an idea with a specific example:

- *Michael's room was a disaster area.* This is a metaphor.
  Suzanne hung her head like a dying flower. This is a simile.
- Magnesium (a metal) burns in oxygen to make Magnesium Oxide (a white powder). $2Mg + O_2 \rightarrow 2MgO$. This is an example of metal combustion. Link symbols to particle model too.

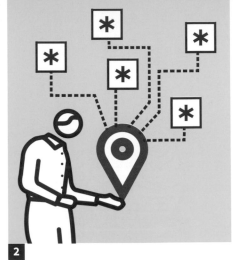

2

DEFINE THE CONCEPT IN GENERAL TERMS

Provide a general definition of the concept or state a general rule that applies in all cases.

- A metaphor is… whereas a simile is… They are similar/different in the following ways…
- The combustion of metals:
  Metal + Oxygen → Metal Oxide. Illustrate this with a general equation.
  $2X + O_2 \rightarrow 2XO$
  or
  $4Y + O_2 \rightarrow 2Y_2O$

Link back to the original example to show how the examples and the general abstract expression or model are connected.

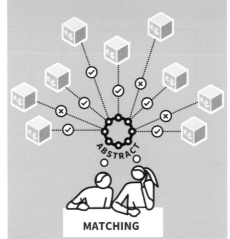

3

PROVIDE FURTHER CONCRETE EXAMPLES

For each abstract concept, provide multiple concrete examples highlighting how the connection works.

- Further examples of metaphors: *The wheels of justice turn slowly. She was all at sea. His face was wooden.*
- Zinc + oxygen → Zinc Oxide
  Iron + oxygen → Iron Oxide
  Carbon + oxygen → Carbon dioxide: Not a metal but the combustion reaction is the same.

4

CHECK FOR UNDERSTANDING

How do different examples fit the general abstract definition? Engage your students in a process where they all have to think about whether some examples match the general pattern. Set tasks that make them generate examples, look for errors, spot the exceptions or the odd-one-out. Engage them in practice activities where they have to categorise examples according to their general abstract characteristics.

5

ENGAGE IN RETRIEVAL PRACTICE

Use the **Concrete Examples** routine so that students can recall and explain specific concrete examples fluently for the concepts they have learned — and vice versa. Students cannot be said to have fully understood what a metaphor is or how a metal reacts with oxygen if they cannot remember any examples. Include concrete example questions in your routine daily, weekly and monthly review activities.

SECTIONS: WHY? | **WHAT?** | HOW?

78

BEHAVIOUR & RELATIONSHIPS | CURRICULUM PLANNING
EXPLAINING & MODELLING | QUESTIONING & FEEDBACK
PRACTICE & RETRIEVAL | MODE B TEACHING

LIVE MODELLING

A central feature of effective instructional teaching is for teachers to walk through a learning process themselves, showing students how to do things, highlighting key procedures and the thinking that underpins them. The metacognitive aspect of modelling is important — making implicit decision-making explicit — as well as providing examples of completed work that can serve as scaffolds for students to base their work on in the initial stages.

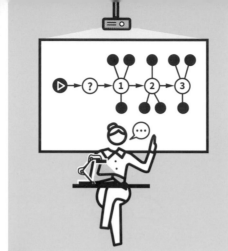

1

MODEL EACH STAGE STEP BY STEP

For any given task, talk through the preliminary thinking. Before starting, narrate the process of thinking through the problem: What is being asked? What information do we already have? What are we aiming to achieve? Then start to undertake the task yourself, talking through each step one action at a time. Use a visualiser or other method to ensure all students see what is being done. They should be listening, not copying at this stage.

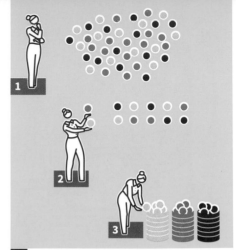

2

MODEL HOW YOU ORGANISE MESSY THINKING

Part of the modelling narrative should include your decision-making process. How do you decide what to do next? If you float three or four possible ideas before selecting one, then model this explicitly. If you go back to edit or improve your work, then model that this is a normal part of the process. If you have a array of ideas, model how you go about putting them into a logical sequence.

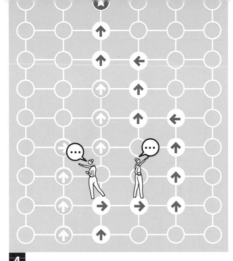

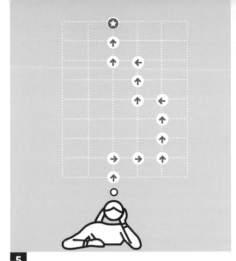

3

REVIEW THE SUCCESS OR QUALITY OF YOUR OWN WORK

Stand back from your modelled example once complete to review it and check for understanding of each step. Evaluate whether your model is correct, complete or meets the success criteria. This models the process students should follow in reviewing their own work. Make this explicit: Have I done it well? Am I correct? Discuss ways it could be improved. If you want students to record your example, this is the moment to do it.

4

MODEL ALTERNATIVES AND FURTHER EXAMPLES

Very often there are multiple possible ways to achieve success and it is important not to confine students' thinking by basing their responses on just one example. It can be important to model multiple alternatives, highlighting how they each meet the success criteria or provide valid alternative routes to success. One example is rarely sufficient to communicate a method or process so providing multiple modelled examples is often important.

5

SET TASKS TO EMULATE THE MODEL

Modelling is just the beginning of the process; it is important that students now try to put the ideas that have been modelled into practice themselves. Initially **Guided Practice** will be important. Then students should move towards **Independent Practice**. At each point, making reference back to the modelled examples will help to keep standards high and to reinforce critical steps in a set procedure.

Attempt | Develop | Adapt | Practise | Test

SECTIONS: WHY? | **WHAT?** | HOW?

80

BEHAVIOUR & RELATIONSHIPS | CURRICULUM PLANNING
EXPLAINING & MODELLING | QUESTIONING & FEEDBACK
PRACTICE & RETRIEVAL | MODE B TEACHING

SCAFFOLDING

One of Rosenshine's Principles of Instruction is based on evidence that more effective teachers provide scaffolds for difficult tasks. Rather than setting lower expectations for students, they support them to reach ambitious goals using a range of scaffolding processes that guide them on the way. Crucially, the metaphor of 'scaffolding' embeds the idea that, when ready, the supports are withdrawn. Scaffolding always comes down; it is only temporary and must not become relied upon in the long run. Designing scaffolds is a key element of curriculum planning.

1

MAP OUT THE COMPONENTS OF A TASK

Break down a task into steps that students will need to follow in order to achieve success. Consider the difficulties that students will encounter moving through the steps and try to design resources that support them to make those steps successfully.

2

PROVIDE SUPPORTS AT A DETAILED LEVEL

Detailed scaffolding might include:
- Word lists
- Diagrams and concept maps or other forms of dual coding.
- Sentence starters or sentence builders
- Useful phrases and connectives
- Prompts for ideas e.g. elements of effective persuasive speeches
- **Knowledge Organisers** setting out key facts
- Exemplars of different elements.

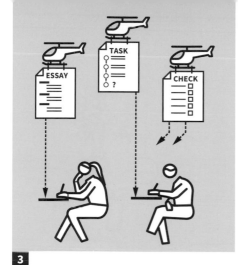

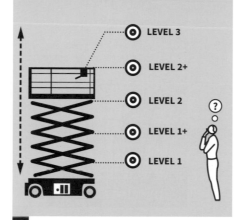

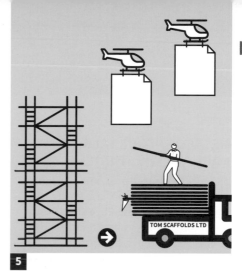

3
PROVIDE SUPPORTS AT OVERVIEW LEVEL

Whole-task scaffolds might include:
- Essay structure strips — with guidelines for a series of paragraphs
- Partially completed examples: started off but not finished
- Partially completed examples: with gaps to fill in throughout
- Checklists of success criteria
- Checking prompts: e.g. Have you checked your fullstops and capital letters?
- Exemplars of completed tasks.

4
PREPARE SCAFFOLDING SETS OFFERING VARYING LEVELS OF SUPPORT

Within a class, set everyone a common goal of producing work to a high standard but give students the level of scaffolding appropriate for their level of confidence. This might vary from maximum scaffolding down to none at all. Sometimes it can work for students to select their own level but this needs careful monitoring in case students over or under pitch the level they are working at.

5
TAKE THE SCAFFOLDING DOWN

The classic sequence in modelling and scaffolding is: I do it; We do it; You do it. I. We. You. The culmination of an instruction and practice phase should be that students attempt a task independently. It's vital that teachers and students know what they are capable of doing unsupported. If the scaffolding has achieved its purpose then this can be a confidence-boosting moment. Choosing when to remove the scaffolds is an important teacher decision.

Attempt | Develop | Adapt | Practise | Test

SECTIONS: WHY? | **WHAT?** | HOW?

82

BEHAVIOUR & RELATIONSHIPS | CURRICULUM PLANNING
EXPLAINING & MODELLING | QUESTIONING & FEEDBACK
PRACTICE & RETRIEVAL | MODE B TEACHING

METACOGNITIVE TALK: NARRATE THE THINKING

It's a well-evidenced phenomenon that successful students also have good metacognitive abilities. They are able to plan, monitor and evaluate their progress through a task; they are able to think strategically about how to go about solving a problem and to articulate their thought processes. Teachers can support students in developing their capacity for metacognitive thinking by modelling it and promoting metacognitive talk in lessons. Essentially, it is a process of narrating thought processes and making them explicit.

See also: **Process Questions**.

WALKTHRUs IN THIS SERIES

EXPLAINING & MODELLING

1

SET A PROBLEM AND EXPLORE IT

Read through the question that has been presented. Focus on establishing what the question is asking or what the task might entail. How is it possible to determine that from the phrasing of the question? It is likely to be related to other familiar and recognisable problem-types so the initial process might be to establish which problem-type it is. This will allow you and students to draw on the relevant past experience and prior knowledge.

2

WHAT DO WE ALREADY KNOW?

Talk through the information that is available in the question and supporting resources. What do we already know from the question? What do we also know from previous learning that might be relevant? Make a list or notes so that this becomes explicit.

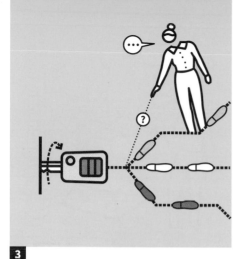

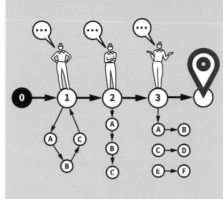

3

WHERE DO WE START?

Talk through the first steps in solving the problem or completing the task. If it is a standard approach that you always take, then stress this so that the routine is established. If there are usually three or four typical starting points from which you choose one, then explore explicitly why you choose a particular option in this case. If it is arbitrary, or if any one path is as good as another, make this explicit. Aim to demystify the whole process.

4

MAKE A PLAN AND MONITOR

Model the process of setting out an overview plan — for example the sequence of steps in a maths problem or the paragraph structure in an essay. Be as explicit as possible about every choice, every step, providing a logical reason for each one.

Then, as you go through the task, narrate your progress through each of the steps. Model the need to check your progress at various stages including an element of time management where that is relevant.

5

HAVE WE BEEN SUCCESSFUL?

When the task has been completed or the problem solved, model the process of self-review, checking back over it to see if it is correct, complete, accurate and finished to a high standard. Explore ways of knowing if an answer is correct within the context of the subject. Checking mechanisms might need to be taught explicitly as part of the curriculum. This might include checking against success criteria, estimation in maths or proof-reading and editing for any form of writing.

SECTIONS: WHY? | **WHAT?** | HOW?

84

BEHAVIOUR & RELATIONSHIPS | CURRICULUM PLANNING
EXPLAINING & MODELLING | QUESTIONING & FEEDBACK
PRACTICE & RETRIEVAL | MODE B TEACHING

SET THE STANDARDS

Dylan Wiliam suggests that, in approaching a learning goal, unless we know where we are going we will never get there. This means that teachers should engage students in a process of clarifying the learning goals. Part of this is to set the standards for the work that will be completed. If students are not aiming for a high standard, they are unlikely to reach it so they need to know what this will look like in advance.

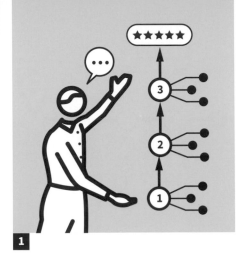

1

MAKE *WHAT DOES EXCELLENCE LOOK LIKE?* A ROUTINE

As an embedded aspect of every instructional process, include a discussion about the nature of excellence in the work that students will produce. This could include the features of excellent writing; an excellent composition; a science practical completed to an excellent standard; a performance in drama or PE that is excellent. Make it so routine that students themselves begin to ask the question.

2

DECONSTRUCT EXEMPLARS

Present exemplars of excellence and engage students in a process of evaluation that allows them all to understand the constituent elements that add up to making the exemplars excellent. This could be pieces of writing, examples of art work, exercise books with excellent presentation; maths solutions that are successful and efficient. It could be performances produced live or recorded from drama, music and PE.

3

CO-CONSTRUCT SUCCESS CRITERIA

Make a list of the features of excellence that emerge from the discussion. These can form success criteria for students' subsequent work. It might be possible to do this without reference to exemplars if the task in hand is definable enough. However, where judgements of quality are involved, make the link from criteria to the exemplars as explicitly as you can.

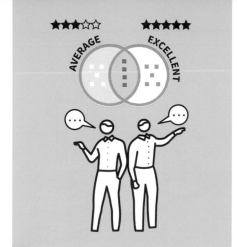

4

REFERENCE CONTRASTING EXEMPLARS

Alongside exemplars of the highest standards, show students exemplars of a range of standards. Explore and discuss the differences supported by **Check for Understanding** routines. Often the differences between an average piece and an excellent piece become clear only when they are compared side by side. This can be much more effective than trying to describe the features of excellence; enable students to see this for themselves.

5

BLEND TEACHER ASSESSMENT AND SELF-ASSESSMENT

When students complete their work, provide feedback referencing the exemplars as a comparison, teasing out key successes and areas for improvement. In doing this you are modelling an assessment process that students can then use themselves.

Ask them to compare their work to the exemplars and identify their own areas of improvement. This helps to deepen their understanding of the standards and develops their capacity for self improvement.

Attempt | Develop | Adapt | Practise | Test

SECTIONS: WHY? | **WHAT?** | HOW?

86

BEHAVIOUR & RELATIONSHIPS | CURRICULUM PLANNING
EXPLAINING & MODELLING | QUESTIONING & FEEDBACK
PRACTICE & RETRIEVAL | MODE B TEACHING

HEAD–ON MISCONCEPTIONS

In many subjects there are several errors or misconceptions that crop up repeatedly. If students have developed a schema around a misconception, it is not sufficient to continually re-teach the correct version because, unless the faulty schema is unpicked, it can remain to surface later. For example you might place a city incorrectly on a map, discover your error but still revert to your faulty map model later — unless you effectively 're-wire' your schema to make the correct version your default. This needs effort and deliberate re-thinking

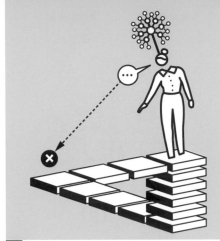

1

IDENTIFY COMMON MISCONCEPTIONS

Use your knowledge of curriculum and assessment in your subject to identify common errors and misconceptions for each topic. Where do students often get stuck or go wrong? Analyse possible underlying reasons for those misconceptions arising. Plan opportunities to teach students about them directly and prepare questions and other resources that explore the misconceptions.

2

INTRODUCE A MISCONCEPTION EXPLICITLY: WHY IS IT WRONG?

Present examples of the misconception to the class, making it clear that the material presented is not fully correct — or is completely wrong:

- Tyler writes: $\frac{1}{4} + \frac{2}{3} = \frac{3}{7}$ What mistake has he made?
- Jennifer says: The candle disappears because the wax has all melted. What was she thinking and why is this wrong?
- Michael says: if 10% of £100 is £10, then 20% of £200 must be £20. What has he done wrong?

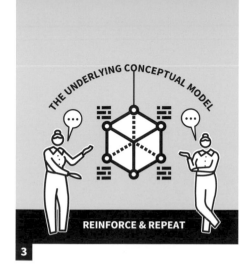

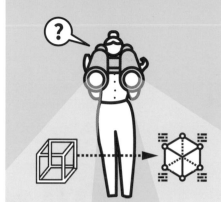

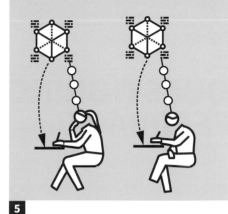

REINFORCE A CORRECT UNDERLYING CONCEPTUAL MODEL

Introduce or re-teach the underlying model that explains why the misconceptions and errors must be wrong. Link this back to the errors that you introduced. It may be necessary to go right back to basics without making any assumptions.

- The need for common denominators when adding fractions.
- Melting and combustion as examples of physical and chemical change.
- The meaning of percentages and ratios.

CHECK FOR UNDERSTANDING OF THE MISCONCEPTION AND THE CORRECTION

Engage students in **Check for Understanding** routines to ensure that they understand both the misconception and the correction. It will not be sufficient to merely talk it through. If your students can explain back to you what the errors are and how to correct them then you can be much more secure about them having understood.

PRACTISE THE CORRECT VERSION

Give students opportunities to strengthen a correct schema through practice. Repeatedly using the ideas that support the corrected schema will help with future recall and will support the process of this becoming the default without reverting back to the misconceptions later. Test students' knowledge and understanding over time by returning to the area where the misconception lies to see if students who previously made mistakes have successfully shifted in their thinking.

QUESTIONING & FEEDBACK

All teachers ask questions and give feedback. However, there can be a significant range in the extent to which these practices have an impact on securing deeper learning with all students in a class. It is important for teachers to develop the capacity to be responsive, adjusting the explanatory inputs and tasks according to how well students are doing in making sense of the material. These WalkThrus set out a repertoire of effective questioning techniques that form the default day-to-day practice in any classroom, enabling a teacher to gain a good sense of how well students are learning. There are also some key feedback techniques that help all students to move forward, deepening their understanding or gaining fluency.

COLD CALLING

Selecting students to answer; involving everyone in thinking

THINK, PAIR, SHARE

A routine for structured discussion

SHOW-ME BOARDS

An effective all-student response technique

CHECK FOR UNDERSTANDING

A key question: What have you understood?

SAY IT AGAIN BETTER

Generating improved verbal responses

PROBING QUESTIONS

Questioning as a set of probing exchanges

PROCESS QUESTIONS

How do we know what we know?

FEEDBACK THAT MOVES FORWARD

Elements of effective formative feedback

FEEDBACK AS ACTIONS

Five ways to make feedback productive

WHOLE-CLASS FEEDBACK

Giving feedback to a whole class at once

SECTIONS: WHY? | **WHAT?** | HOW?

90

BEHAVIOUR & RELATIONSHIPS | CURRICULUM PLANNING
EXPLAINING & MODELLING | **QUESTIONING & FEEDBACK**
PRACTICE & RETRIEVAL | MODE B TEACHING

COLD CALLING

This technique helps to address the two main purposes of questioning: making all students think and providing feedback to you as the teacher as to how well things are going. If you are to gain a reasonable idea of how well students have understood the material in hand, it is important to involve them all in thinking and then to sample responses strategically. If you allow 'hands up' or calling out, you only get responses from volunteers. This quickly becomes the norm. Cold calling allows you to choose who answers, keeping the whole class involved and giving you better information from which to plan your next responsive steps.

WALKTHRUs IN THIS SERIES

QUESTIONING & FEEDBACK

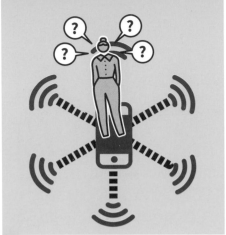

1

ASK THE CLASS THE QUESTION

The best approach is to ask a question aimed at everyone in the room. This then gives everyone a chance to consider the answer, checking their own recall and understanding. If you use a range of techniques, you might want to name the approach. "OK everyone, we'll cold call this question: What are the main reasons for …? "This tells everyone that you will not accept hands up and that calling out is not acceptable. It also tells students to be prepared to give their answers.

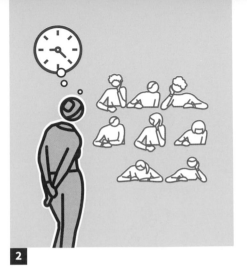

2

GIVE THINKING TIME

Allow students time to think in silence before seeking responses. This could be anything from 5–30 seconds or perhaps longer depending on the complexity. This is especially important for anything beyond simple recall questions where shorter response times might be more appropriate. Use the thinking time to scan the room, checking students are focusing on the task, as far as you can tell.

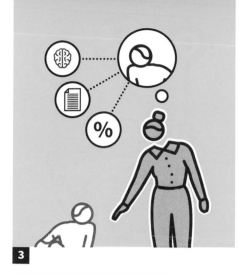

3

SELECT SOMEONE TO RESPOND

Using your knowledge of the students, select a student to respond. The idea is that this could be anyone including someone you have only recently asked. Using names tells them that you are interested in each respondent and their ideas. It can be helpful to ask a diffusing question such as "James, what were you thinking?" which invites James to present his half-formed thoughts or to say that he wasn't sure. If we over-stress correctness at an early stage, this can inhibit less confident students. Make it safe for errors, doubts and misconceptions to surface.

4

RESPOND TO THE ANSWERS

Try to turn each question into a short exchange. If a good answer is given, respond with an affirmation and a **Probing Question** or a **Process Question**. "Yes, that's really good — which method did you use?" Or "And can you give me another example?". If the answer isn't quite right, respond with something like "Good try… but that's not quite right…" before re-teaching or giving a prompt either directly or via another student. Very often the **Say It Again Better** strategy is useful as a response.

5

SELECT ANOTHER STUDENT AND RESPOND AGAIN

After the first exchange, invite another student to respond to the exact same question or a slight extension of the original question. Choose a range of students including those who are enthusiastic about answering and those who are less confident and would tend to opt out. Scan the room making sure all students know that they too could be asked. Repeat the response process each time until you feel you've received enough feedback to decide to proceed or to re-teach.

Attempt | Develop | Adapt | Practise | Test

SECTIONS: WHY? | **WHAT?** | HOW?

92

BEHAVIOUR & RELATIONSHIPS | CURRICULUM PLANNING
EXPLAINING & MODELLING | **QUESTIONING & FEEDBACK**
PRACTICE & RETRIEVAL | MODE B TEACHING

THINK, PAIR, SHARE

There are many times during a learning sequence when it is beneficial for students to engage in a structured discussion. Pairs are the most powerful way to involve all students in rehearsing and sharing ideas as part of the flow of responsive teaching. Used well, in conjunction with **Signal, Pause, Insist**, teachers can switch from whole-class listening and back to paired discussion in a dynamic orderly routine providing all students the opportunity to talk about the material in hand in a productive manner.

1

ESTABLISH TALK PARTNERS FOR EVERY STUDENT

If this is a strategy you use repeatedly, it is useful to pre-determine each person's talk partner. Odd students can form the one group of three. Ideally pairs will be reasonably well matched so that one person in the pair does not dominate each discussion and do all the thinking.

2

SET THE QUESTION WITH A GOAL AND A TIMEFRAME

In the same style as **Cold Calling**, set a question for all students to discuss in their pairs. You may want a free discussion to generate ideas but it is often helpful to set a precise goal to focus the time e.g. *"List five key features of the character"; "Explain the process in four or five bullet points", "Name all six parts of the structure"*. Along with the question, set a precise timeframe. This makes the short discussions purposeful and energetic. e.g. *"You've got three minutes to explain the method to Question 7"*.

3

BUILD IN THINKING TIME

An optional feature of this process is to give students time to think individually before they turn to their talk partners to share their ideas. The advantage of this is that it makes sure every member of the class engages in generative thinking before their partner offers their ideas. The disadvantage is that it can take up more time so you might decide to go straight to the discussion.

4

CIRCULATE TO LISTEN AS PAIRS ARE TALKING

Very often the power of this technique lies in hearing what students say to each other, circulating around the class as they share ideas in their pairs. This can help to pick up particularly interesting ideas or important errors, misconceptions or subtle technicalities. It also helps to keep the discussions focused. This is more relevant when more extended in-depth questions have been asked.

5

USE COLD CALL TO SAMPLE PAIRS' RESPONSES

At the end of the time, use **Signal Pause Insist** to bring the class to attention. Sample the discussions by choosing who to respond, as with **Cold Calling**. Again, give them the option to reveal their doubts as well as any ideas. *"Michael, what were you and Annie discussing in your pair?"*. This means Annie can't talk for Michael but he can either give an extended response or express uncertainty. Then select other pairs to contribute their ideas or **Check for Understanding**.

SECTIONS: WHY? | **WHAT?** | HOW?

94   BEHAVIOUR & RELATIONSHIPS | CURRICULUM PLANNING
EXPLAINING & MODELLING | **QUESTIONING & FEEDBACK**
PRACTICE & RETRIEVAL | MODE B TEACHING

SHOW–ME BOARDS

A good way to sample the responses from a whole class is to use mini-whiteboards. (MWBs). These can be called 'Show–Me' boards, highlighting the way they are used. They are cheap to buy and can become part of the standard equipment in any classroom. The basic idea is that students write on the boards in response to a question and then, simultaneously, show the teacher their responses, giving a big hit of feedback to the teacher about the range of responses around the class. They also help where you want students to generate ideas or practise making diagrams or short sentences.

1

2

ENSURE EVERY STUDENT HAS A BOARD AND PEN TO HAND

Ideally they should be ready to use whenever you choose to use them spontaneously, not a big deal to borrow or organise in advance. It can help to have sets of board+pen+wiper in wallets to speed up the logistics of handing them out.

SET THE QUESTION WITH A GOAL AND A TIMEFRAME

Ask students to produce the particular type of response you want with clear goals e.g. to write out the maths solutions, to sketch a diagram, to write out a balanced chemical equation, to write the sentence with the correct grammar, to describe the main features of the poem or piece of music. Give students a timeframe for the task in minutes.

WALKTHRUs IN THIS SERIES

QUESTIONING & FEEDBACK

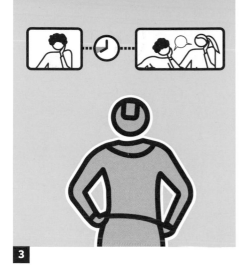

3

BUILD IN THINKING TIME

Before students are allowed to show their responses, make sure every student has had time to think, exploring their own schema. It can interrupt their thinking if another student's answer is shared prematurely.

4

SIGNAL: 3–2–1 AND SHOW ME

Use a crisp, disciplined routine that makes every student show their boards at the same time. When the time limit has been reached, signal *"3-2-1 and Show Me"* — or a similar signal. This is an instruction for students to stop writing and hold up their boards for you to see the responses. They should keep the boards held up for as long as you need to absorb the responses and use them to inform your next steps.

5

SAMPLE STUDENT RESPONSES AND FOLLOW UP

The purpose of this process is to give you feedback so, after scanning the boards for correct and incorrect responses, interesting alternative responses, common errors or misconceptions, engage with a sample of students to discuss their responses, either to consolidate, deepen or correct as needed. Combine with **Probing Questions** and **Check for Understanding.**

SECTIONS: WHY? | **WHAT?** | HOW?

96

BEHAVIOUR & RELATIONSHIPS | CURRICULUM PLANNING
EXPLAINING & MODELLING | **QUESTIONING & FEEDBACK**
PRACTICE & RETRIEVAL | MODE B TEACHING

CHECK FOR UNDERSTANDING

A central idea in Rosenshine's Principles of Instruction is that more effective teachers will systematically check for understanding from their students. We can't assume students have understood words, ideas, concepts, explanations or procedures unless we get some feedback from them, telling us what they have understood. The information we receive by checking should inform the next steps in a learning sequence: to re-teach some material, tackle misconceptions or perhaps move on more quickly to new material. The checking process itself also helps students to secure deeper understanding.

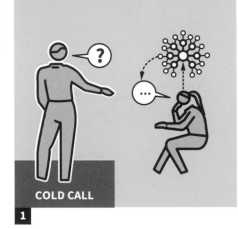

COLD CALL

1

COLD CALL, ASKING *WHAT*, NOT *IF*

After teacher input or a practice episode, select a student to share their thinking. *"Louisa ,what have you understood?"* This is a much better question than asking *"Has everyone understood?"* or *"Louisa, do you understand?"* which are unlikely to yield helpful responses. Louisa now has to construct a response that shows what she has understood about the question in hand, helping her to develop the knowledge in her long-term memory and providing feedback to the teacher.

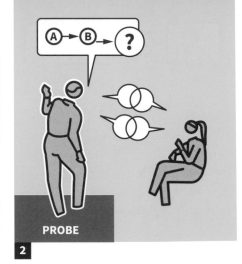

PROBE

2

PROBE WITH A SHORT DIALOGUE

Go beyond accepting a short response. Use **Probing Questions** and **Process Questions** to find out more about what the student thinks, checking that they have understood the material in hand. *"That's interesting; what other reasons could there be; which of those features is the most important; what would happen next; is there another way you could express the same idea?"*

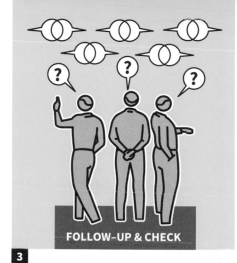

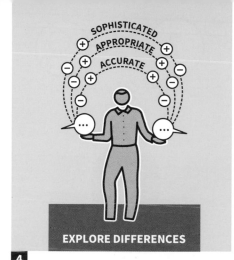

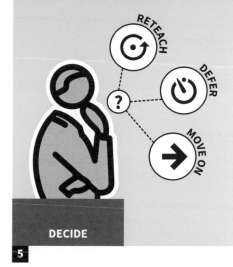

FOLLOW–UP & CHECK

3

EXPLORE DIFFERENCES

4

DECIDE

5

FOLLOW-UP WITH MORE CHECKING DIALOGUES

After one student has responded, select another student and repeat the process. They should answer the same question or a developed version, using their previous thinking combined with ideas gleaned from the previous teacher-student exchange. Again, probe to make sure they've properly understood, supporting them as needed. Select a third person to give yet another explanation. This is often sufficient but you can select more students to respond if you're looking for a wider range of responses, particularly if the material is very challenging or open-ended.

EXPLORE DIFFERENCES AND DETAILS

Very often there is rich material in exploring differences between student explanations. Which answer is more accurate, appropriate or sophisticated? Are there any errors or misconceptions? Have words and concepts been used correctly? Is each alternative answer equally valid?

RE-TEACH, DEFER OR MOVE ON

Using your knowledge of the students and the material in hand, decide whether students seem to have understood to sufficient depth. If they have, move on or elect to give more challenging questions. If they have not, go back to re-teach key aspects or provide more practice. You might also choose to defer a re-teaching phase to a future lesson, perhaps after asking students to review or practise independently in the meantime.

Attempt | Develop | Adapt | Practise | Test

SECTIONS; WHY? | **WHAT?** | HOW?

98

BEHAVIOUR & RELATIONSHIPS | CURRICULUM PLANNING
EXPLAINING & MODELLING | **QUESTIONING & FEEDBACK**
PRACTICE & RETRIEVAL | MODE B TEACHING

SAY IT AGAIN BETTER

The purpose of this technique is to set a standard for the depth of verbal responses you expect from students and to support them to produce high quality responses. If you accept short, shallow responses without further development, it sets low expectations and students will assume half-formed answers are the norm. However, unless you allow students to initially offer their more basic ideas, you can deter them from trying to answer in future. With **Say It Again Better**, you accept initial responses but develop them each time.

1

ASK A STUDENT A QUESTION

Use one of the questioning techniques to invite students to think about the material in hand and to prepare to respond. This might include:

- **Cold Calling**
- **Think Pair Share**
- **Check for Understanding.**

The more complex the material and the demanding the question, the more important this technique will be.

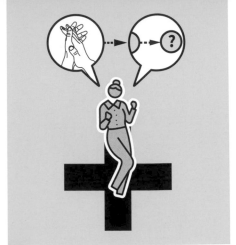

2

ACKNOWLEDGE THE FIRST RESPONSE

When a student you have selected gives a response, be as positive as possible about their offering. If it is a half-formed answer, falling short of what might be an excellent response, say something like: *"Yes, OK, that's a good start. But let's develop it further"*. If they are simply wrong, say something like *"Good try but that's not quite it; let's see how we can get it right"*.

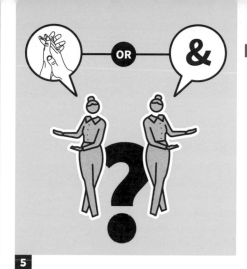

3

GIVE SUPPORTIVE FORMATIVE FEEDBACK

Invite the student to consider specific ways in which the response could be improved.

- What's the more formal/technical term for that idea?
- Does the graph just 'go up' or is there a more complex pattern you could describe?
- Can you include a reason for that opinion to back it up — remember we should be aiming for *"I believe X is true because…."*

4

INVITE STUDENT TO "SAY IT AGAIN BETTER"

After exploring what a better answer might include, ask the same student to have another attempt, *"OK, now try to say it again better"*. This is important because in giving the improved answer, you can check that they've understood at the same time as giving them an opportunity for practice and for feeling more successful having generated a higher quality response.

5

RESPOND TO THE IMPROVED RESPONSE

Decide if the improved response is sufficiently improved to warrant simple affirmative praise before moving on or whether there is value in adding more detail or depth or accuracy. You can repeat the feedback process and then ask for a further response that is even better still. The effect of this process is to demonstrate to students that they are capable of excellent responses and in time it is likely to become more common for them to produce them first time around.

Attempt | Develop | Adapt | Practise | Test

SECTIONS: WHY? | **WHAT?** | HOW?

100

BEHAVIOUR & RELATIONSHIPS | CURRICULUM PLANNING
EXPLAINING & MODELLING | **QUESTIONING & FEEDBACK**
PRACTICE & RETRIEVAL | MODE B TEACHING

PROBING QUESTIONS

In order to develop students' understanding it is important to ask questions that make them probe their schema for the ideas being discussed. Well-chosen questions can support students to make links between ideas, to rehearse explanations to support long-term memory, to connect abstract and concrete examples and to identify knowledge gaps and misconceptions. Probing questioning can be a one-off technique but might develop into a habitual questioning style.

WALKTHRUs IN THIS SERIES

QUESTIONING & FEEDBACK

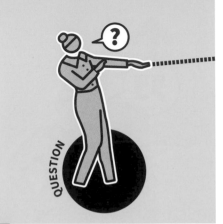

1

ASK A STUDENT A QUESTION

Use one of the questioning techniques to invite students to think about the material in hand and to prepare to respond. This might include

- **Cold Calling**
- **Think Pair Share**
- **Check for Understanding.**

The more complex the material and the demanding the question, the more important this technique will be.

2

FOLLOW–UP WITH A PROBING QUESTION

Probing questions might include:

- *What's the connection between A and B?*
- *Is that always true or just in this case?*
- *Is there another example?*
- *What are the main reasons?*
- *What would be the most important factor?*
- *If we change variable C, what happens to variable D?*
- *How does that idea explain this phenomenon?*

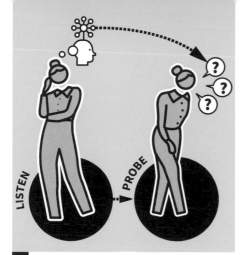

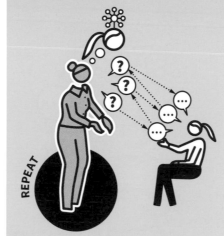

3

LISTEN AND PROBE FURTHER

Continue exploring the student's schema, listening carefully and responding accordingly.

- *OK, so if that's true what about this?*
- *Is there another way you can explain it?*
- *What else could you add to explain the variation?*
- *If A is true and B is false, what might we say about C?*
- *In what ways is that similar or different to the previous example?*

4

ASK ANOTHER STUDENT TO CONTINUE

Once you have completed 3, 4 or 5 exchanges with the first student, repeat steps 1–3, selecting another student and probing their schema.

The rhythm of the questioning between Teacher T and students A, B and C might be:

- T-A-T-A-T-A
- T-B-T-B-T-B-T-B
- T-C-T-C-T-C

Each student engages in a probing exchange.

5

CHECK FOR UNDERSTANDING FROM OTHERS

After a probing exchange, select other students to **Check for Understanding.**

- *What did you understand from Joe's response?*
- *Do you agree more with Michael or Safia?*

These questions are useful as a check for student and teacher but they also support the idea that all students should listen in when a probing dialogue is taking place and be ready to engage themselves.

SECTIONS: WHY? | **WHAT?** | HOW?

102

BEHAVIOUR & RELATIONSHIPS | CURRICULUM PLANNING
EXPLAINING & MODELLING | **QUESTIONING & FEEDBACK**
PRACTICE & RETRIEVAL | MODE B TEACHING

PROCESS QUESTIONS

In Rosenshine's Principles of Instruction he suggests that more effective teachers typically ask process questions in their repertoire whereas less effective teachers might not ask any at all. Similarly, the EEF guidance report on metacognition, suggests teachers should encourage metacognitive talk during lessons. In both, this means that discussions focus on questions such as *'how do we know'* or *'how do we work it out?'* Modelling and rehearing dialogue around these questions supports students to develop the capacity to think in this way independently within the same subject area.

1

MODEL YOUR THINKING

During any instructional phase of a lesson narrate your thought processes explicitly. As you talk through a problem, question or writing task, make your thinking explicit, including where you:

- draw on recall of knowledge or previous examples
- make arbitrary choices or use trial and error
- use a strategy that should always be used as a routine
- plan key ideas before writing about each one
- check your own answers for accuracy

HOW
WHY

2

EMPHASISE *HOW* AND *WHY*

During an instructional exchange, routinely place an emphasis on how we know what we know and why the answer is the answer as far as possible. It is important, for example, to show that we might learn that 7-squared is 49 as a number fact — we learn it by heart. But we probably work out 7-cubed by multiplying 49 by 7.

This could be done in various ways e.g.
$7 \times 50 = 350$ so 7×49 is $350 - 7 = 343$
or
$7 \times 40 = 280$; $7 \times 9 = 63$; $280 + 63 = 343$.

3

ASK STUDENTS TO EXPLAIN THEIR METHODS AND REASONING

When a student has given a response , follow up with a process question:

- *Thanks, James, that's correct — what method did you use?*
- *That's interesting, Sherin — why did you put them in that order?*
- *That's not quite right, Nazrin — what were you assuming about factor B?*

OR

4

ASK STUDENTS TO EXPLAIN THEIR IDEAS AND CHOICES

When students are asked to volunteer ideas of select an option from a set of choices, ask them to justify them:

- *Great idea, Taran. What made you think of that?*
- *Interesting suggestion, Alice. Why do you think that would work?*
- *Wow, great example, Lisa. Where did that idea come from?*

5

ASK HOW SIMILAR ALTERNATIVE QUESTIONS OR PROBLEMS MIGHT BE APPROACHED

It's important to reinforce divergent and evaluative thinking; to show how a range of approaches can be valid even if some are better than others.

- *Naureen, can you suggest a different way of approaching this question?*
- *Is there another way we could explain Macbeth's response? Andy?*
- *Is there another way to start the sentence to make it more emphatic? Robin?*

Attempt | Develop | Adapt | **Practise** | Test

SECTIONS: WHY? | **WHAT?** | HOW?

104 BEHAVIOUR & RELATIONSHIPS | CURRICULUM PLANNING
EXPLAINING & MODELLING | **QUESTIONING & FEEDBACK**
PRACTICE & RETRIEVAL | MODE B TEACHING

FEEDBACK THAT MOVES FORWARD

Feedback plays a central role in securing students' learning, supporting them to know how to deepen their knowledge and understanding or improve their performance. However, it's important to recognise that, in order for feedback to be effective, it needs to be understood and accepted and to be actionable so that students can use it to secure improvements in their knowledge and performance at a later time. Part of this relies on feedback providing motivation to apply effort alongside specifics of the strategies they need to employ.

WALKTHRUs IN THIS SERIES

QUESTIONING & FEEDBACK

1

FOCUS FORWARDS

Use formal and informal assessments to identify areas for improvement in students' performance or gaps in their understanding. However, rather than trying to describe their past performance, focus on describing actions they can take to improve future performance. Crucially this requires there to be an opportunity to make improvements so feedback needs to be given part-way through a learning cycle, not at the end.

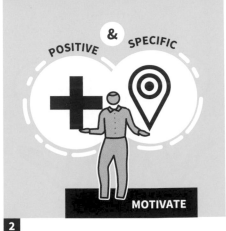

2

KEEP IT POSITIVE AND SPECIFIC

In order to be motivating and actionable, feedback should largely be framed in language that is positive and encouraging. Tell students the things they are succeeding at that they should continue to reinforce alongside the things they can do differently. Be as specific as possible so that students receiving the feedback know what to do in response. e.g. Rather than suggesting a student should 'write a better conclusion', specify how the conclusion could be improved.

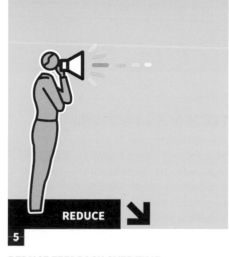

NURTURE OR **PUSH**

3

NO SATNAV

4

REDUCE

5

MATCH THE MESSAGE TO THE STUDENT

Feedback only succeeds if students trust it and use it to increase their effort or raise their aspirations and, as a result, improve their performance. Remember that different students respond in complex ways. Some need careful nurturing and respond badly to perceived criticism. Others need a strong push to lead them to increase their effort whilst soft feedback makes them complacent. Learn how each student typically responds to feedback as a key feature of your relationship-building.

AVOID SATNAV SYNDROME

A SatNav system gives continuous directions making it possible to travel from A to B without ever learning the route. Give your feedback focusing on changing students' capacity to produce excellent work and less on producing a specific exemplary piece. Give prompts and clues but leave students to take improvement steps independently, making them think about what is needed, not simply following step by step instructions. Include **Process Questions** in feedback discussions.

REDUCE FEEDBACK OVER TIME

As students engage in **Independent Practice** and gain confidence, reduce the detail in the feedback given, allowing more struggle time before offering feedback. In general, train students to generate as much self-assessed feedback as possible referencing success criteria, exemplars of standards, study guides and worked answers as needed.

SECTIONS: WHY? | **WHAT?** | HOW?

106   BEHAVIOUR & RELATIONSHIPS | CURRICULUM PLANNING
EXPLAINING & MODELLING | **QUESTIONING & FEEDBACK**
PRACTICE & RETRIEVAL | MODE B TEACHING

FEEDBACK AS ACTIONS

If feedback is to move students forward in their learning, it can be helpful to frame it as an instruction to do something. This can be more useful and easier to understand than focusing on describing work that has been done previously. In giving feedback as actions, students are being set a task that addresses their learning needs; the feedback is embedded in the selection of the task.

This WalkThru is not five consecutive steps; it is a list of five possible alternatives to consider.

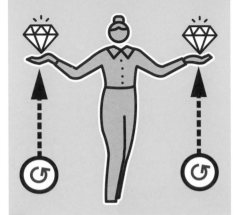

1

REDRAFT OR RE–DO

Give opportunities to improve a piece of work by repeating it one or more times, taking on board ideas about how the work could be done to a higher standard. These ideas might come from **Whole-Class Feedback**, specific actionable comments or by giving students exemplar work to compare to their own. Sometimes it's enough just to say 'do it again better' with students generating their own ideas about how to improve.

2

REHEARSE OR REPEAT

Ask students to focus on certain aspects of learning that they have already encountered with a view to improve their confidence and fluency. This might include repeating sets of maths problems, using phrases in French or rehearsing explanations or performances. Improvement through repetition and rehearsal can be secured in a range of subject contexts.

3

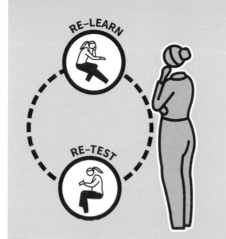

4

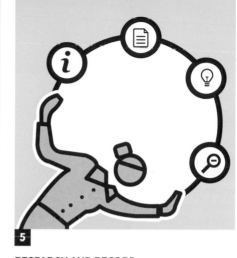

5

REVISIT AND RESPOND TO MORE QUESTIONS

Instead of going back to make corrections on a complex array of previous questions, it can be more productive and efficient to re-teach some key elements where common errors were occurring and then set a fresh set of questions to respond to. The feedback is essentially "do these questions". In doing so, the key aspects of feedback are being acted on.

RE-LEARN MATERIAL AND RE-TEST

Where students have been required to learn a specific set of knowledge but have gaps in their recall, the feedback can be to identify which specific details they found hard to recall and to engage in one or more specific retrieval practice activities. If the knowledge and the retrieval technique are very specific, this works well as feedback.

RESEARCH AND RECORD

Where students' work would be improved by making reference to a wider range of ideas, texts, case studies, examples or contain more details, the feedback can be that they should do some focused research online or from specific books and record their findings. They should then try to reference these new ideas in an improved version of the task.

Attempt | Develop | Adapt | Practise | Test

SECTIONS: WHY? | **WHAT?** | HOW?

108

BEHAVIOUR & RELATIONSHIPS | CURRICULUM PLANNING
EXPLAINING & MODELLING | **QUESTIONING & FEEDBACK**
PRACTICE & RETRIEVAL | MODE B TEACHING

WHOLE-CLASS FEEDBACK

As part of a diet of feedback of various kinds, this technique is an excellent way to give students timely, detailed formative feedback whilst minimising teacher workload. It replaces writing individual comments in books with feedback given to the class as a whole. This allows the teacher to engage with the details of the work students produce rapidly, to inform a short, effective feedback and improvement cycle. Some teachers use a template to record the feedback; others just use more organic notes.

1

READ THROUGH STUDENTS' WORK

After collecting in a set of books, read through them, focusing on specific recent pieces of work or just one. It's important that this happens before the next time you will see the students so that, in giving the feedback, it forms part of the flow of ideas in your teaching sequence and students have good recall of doing the work concerned. Ideally read all the books but, if time is pressing, a sample can be sufficient.

2

NOTE THE STRENGTHS

Identify common areas of strength and write them down. When reporting back to students it will help to stress the things that are being done well so that they are reinforced as well as serving as a prompt to the few students not yet doing them. Identify a small number of specific examples of excellent work with the intention of showcasing them as models in the feedback.

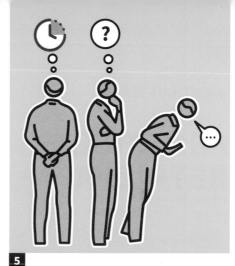

3
NOTE AREAS FOR IMPROVEMENT

Reading through, make a manageable list of common misconceptions, spelling errors, technical errors and any other areas for improvement. It's reasonable to assume that any error you spot is worth sharing as a learning point with the class. As the feedback will be public, don't attach errors to individuals. However, note any individuals who you feel you might need to speak to individually because of specific issues.

4
GIVE THE FEEDBACK

The next lesson, give the work back and present the feedback to the whole class, running over the strengths and areas for improvement. This can be done via a one-slide presentation or, using a visualiser to show your notes. You might copy the feedback sheet to give to each student as a record but this is not required every time; it can make the process more time consuming. Take time to highlight the examples of excellence, using a visualiser, a photo or other appropriate showcase method.

5
GIVE IMPROVEMENT TIME

As soon as you have given the feedback, give students some time in the lesson to make immediate improvements. They need to identify where in their work the common errors occur and where they have improvements to make in line with the feedback given. This will make them think hard about the quality of their own work and can foster a stronger understanding of standards. Offer to provide clarification as needed. Seek out individuals for one-to-one conversations about their work.

Attempt | Develop | Adapt | Practise | Test

PRACTICE & RETRIEVAL

This selection of WalkThrus explores various strategies that overlap strongly with Rosenshine's Principles of Instruction and Willingham's ideas about fluency and drilling. Students can improve their confidence and fluency with a wide range of knowledge and physical skills through engaging in practice, starting with closely supervised guided practice before moving on to practise more independently. An aspect of this is the role retrieval practice plays in securing students' fluency in storing and retrieving information from their long-term memory, tackling the ever-present problem that forgetting is all too easy. We are keen to stress that retrieval practice takes many forms; there's a lot more to it than a set of quizzes, even though quizzing can be very useful. In general, fluency in retrieval is a very useful idea in teaching and we have selected a number of techniques for building fluency that involve every student in a class.

QUIZZING
PAGE 112

Steps for running effective quizzing routines

ELABORATIVE INTERROGATION
PAGE 114

Exploring schema with Why and How questions

USING A KNOWLEDGE ORGANISER
PAGE 116

Resources to support students' knowledge checking

REHEARSAL & PERFORMANCE
PAGE 118

The power of rehearsal in practising for performance

PEER–SUPPORTED RETRIEVAL
PAGE 120

Using students as resources for each other

WEEKLY & MONTHLY REVIEW
PAGE 122

Routine knowledge checking to reduce forgetting

CONCRETE EXAMPLES
PAGE 124

Linking concrete examples to abstract ideas

GUIDED PRACTICE
PAGE 126

Securing early success with supervised practice

INDEPENDENT PRACTICE
PAGE 128

Letting students go to practise on their own

BUILDING FLUENCY
PAGE 130

Building from drills into more complex tasks

SECTIONS: WHY? | **WHAT?** | HOW?

112

BEHAVIOUR & RELATIONSHIPS | CURRICULUM PLANNING
EXPLAINING & MODELLING | QUESTIONING & FEEDBACK
PRACTICE & RETRIEVAL | MODE B TEACHING

QUIZZING

A simple routine knowledge quiz helps to check that students have learned the material you want to them to know. The process of quizzing provides information to both student and teacher about what has been learned and where gaps still exist. In addition, the process of being tested reinforces the retrieval strength of the material so that it is easier to remember later. Quizzing can become a form of practice. With well-planned quizzing providing a balance of intensity and spaced practice over time, students will be able to remember the information more fluently.

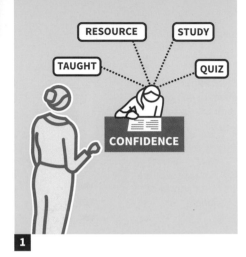

1

SPECIFY THE MATERIAL IN ADVANCE

Make sure that the material that will be the focus of future quizzing has already been taught and that students have the resource — they can use it to study form in advance. If students perceive that quiz questions cannot be prepared for through study, they might not apply the necessary effort to studying the material. A good quiz should support the principle of building confidence with every student aiming at a high success rate.

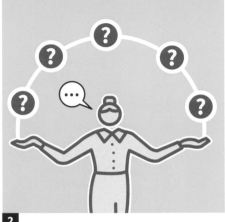

2

ASK A SET OF SHORT FACTUAL RECALL QUESTIONS, VARYING IN STYLE

For any given set of knowledge, ask 5-10 questions checking for recall in a variety of styles including:

- Short answer fact check
- Short problem solving — e.g. using maths facts
- Multiple Choice questions
- True/False or error spotting
- Labelling diagrams/image recognition
- Recitation of quotes or definitions.
- Short bullet-point lists. Of course longer quizzes are an option, depending on the purpose, intended difficulty and time available.

3

4

5

GIVE ALL STUDENTS TIME TO ANSWER ALL OF THE QUESTIONS

Ideally the goal is to check that all students know all the material in question. This requires that a quiz allows all students to answer all the questions, not giving them a selection or hearing answers before they've been able to check their own recall. Depending on the nature of the questions, they can be done as mini paper test, asked verbally one by one or presented all at once for students to answer in their own time.

PROVIDE THE ANSWERS FOR STUDENTS TO SELF OR PEER-CHECK

Once the students have completed the quiz, provide the answers for them to check. The most time-efficient process is to reveal all answers simultaneously on a slide or visualiser. However, it may be necessary to provide an explanation for each answer and to cover them one by one. The key is that students can see or hear the answers so they can compare their own for accuracy. Peer checking is a useful alternative — swapping answer sheets between pairs of students.

AFFIRM GOOD PERFORMANCE AND SEEK OUT WRONG ANSWERS

In addition to the retrieval practice itself, the most useful outcome from a quiz is that each student learns where they have gaps in their knowledge and the teacher learns what the common gaps are. After answers have been checked give affirmative praise for good overall performance but also take time to ask students for examples of questions they got wrong. Explore the reasons, re-teaching as needed. Do as much of this as the time allows.

Attempt | Develop | Adapt | Practise | Test

SECTIONS: WHY? | **WHAT?** | HOW?

114

BEHAVIOUR & RELATIONSHIPS | CURRICULUM PLANNING
EXPLAINING & MODELLING | QUESTIONING & FEEDBACK
PRACTICE & RETRIEVAL | MODE B TEACHING

ELABORATIVE INTERROGATION

In this process, the aim is for students to explore the links and connections within their schema for a set of knowledge by asking Why?, How? and What happens next? questions. Research shows that students can improve their long-term retention and deepen their understanding if a peer asks them elaborative interrogative questions or if they mentally interrogate themselves using the same style of questions.

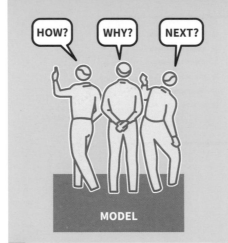

1

MODEL HOW TO GENERATE HOW, WHY AND WHAT NEXT QUESTIONS

Model the process of elaborative interrogation explicitly, showing students the way different question stems lead to different types of response:

- How does…? Explanations of processes.
- Why did…? Explorations of reasoning, cause and effect; rationale and motivation.
- What happens if…? Explorations of variables and their effects, making predictions using a model.

2

EITHER USE PAIRED ELABORATIVE INTERROGATION

Allocate students to quiz each other in pairs. It is likely that the students asking the questions will need a resource to help them, prompting deeper questions. They should ask a series of elaborative interrogative questions. The students answering should be encouraged to give answers that are as expansive as possible, not simple one word, one line responses. Stress the value of exploring chains of connections within their schema.

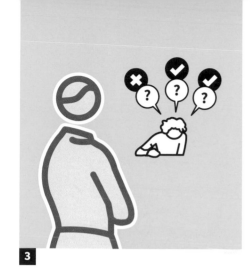

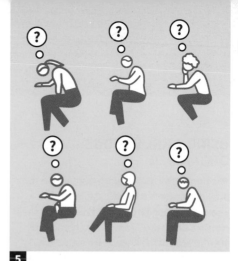

3

OR USE INDIVIDUAL ELABORATIVE INTERROGATION

Set time for students to engage in silent individual elaborative interrogation, testing their own knowledge. The idea is that they generate their own questions and answer them themselves. In a class context, this is hidden from the teacher, so it can be important for students to know that a follow-up process will require them to demonstrate their knowledge. This will add a degree of accountability to the process, motivating students to think hard about good questions and good answers in their heads.

4

CHECK FOR ACCURACY

Ensure that wherever possible and necessary, students in pairs provide corrective feedback to their partners, referencing a resource to ensure their feedback is accurate. Where students engage in a period of self-interrogation, they should refer to their notes or sources to check the accuracy of their recall. This is important so that subsequent consolidation and recall is more accurate and detailed.

5

CONSOLIDATE WITH QUIZZING OR OTHER FORMS OF ASSESSMENT

Elaborative interrogation has strong potential for supporting schema-building but because it is largely hidden from the teacher, it is useful to provide further opportunities to demonstrate the results in some other form of assessment.

Self-interrogation can be a useful preparation for a written test or assessment or performance. Teachers can try to infer from students' performance whether their retrieval strategies are effective.

SECTIONS: WHY? | **WHAT?** | HOW?

116

BEHAVIOUR & RELATIONSHIPS | CURRICULUM PLANNING
EXPLAINING & MODELLING | QUESTIONING & FEEDBACK
PRACTICE & RETRIEVAL | MODE B TEACHING

USING A KNOWLEDGE ORGANISER

The purpose of a knowledge organiser is to provide students with accessible guidance about knowledge that they can study on their own in order to build a secure schema with strong recall of the knowledge elements. They are intended as a summary; not a comprehensive, exhaustive list of all that could be known. However, they only serve a purpose if they are used effectively, linked to retrieval techniques.

WALKTHRUs IN THIS SERIES

PRACTICE AND RETRIEVAL

1

DESIGN KNOWLEDGE ORGANISERS TO BE QUIZZABLE

Present the key information you want students to learn in a format that supports self-quizzing. Avoid using extended prose and ensure information is clearly visible. Useful features include:

- Tables with columns of related information allowing one or more columns to be covered.
- Bullet point lists of key ideas
- Sequences shown in flow diagrams
- Labelled and unlabelled versions of diagrams
- Clear mindmaps or timelines

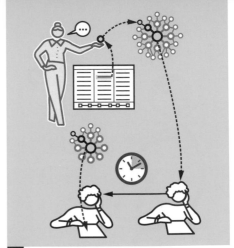

2

FOCUS ON SPECIFIC ELEMENTS

Typically, knowledge organisers span much more information than can be quizzed on sensibly at any one time. Direct students to read specific elements in advance of any retrieval practice activities whilst highlighting how the section fits into a bigger schema of knowledge. It's important that a quizzing process supports building connections rather than isolating facts and ideas such that they lose meaning.

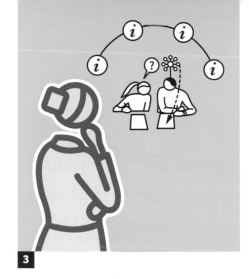

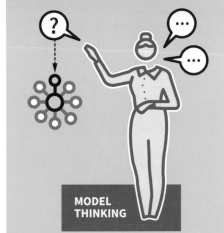

MODEL THINKING

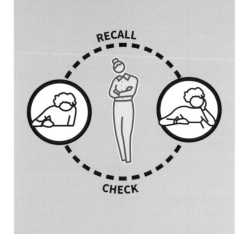

RECALL

CHECK

3

READ AND REHEARSE

Ask students to read through their knowledge organiser including saying all the words, reading through equations and tracking through any charts, flow diagrams or pictorial representations. Rehearse using the organiser by asking questions based on the content whilst students are still looking at it. Then ask them to do this themselves or in pairs so they are engaging with the information beyond merely staring at it. They need to focus on meaning and content, beyond any visual representation.

4

CLOSE OR COVER FOR GENERATIVE RECALL

This is the active step. Students need to remove the information from view and then engage in a generative recall process: completing a table, listing the bullet points, adding labels to a diagram, placing ideas in the correct sequence, remembering definitions.

Teachers can support this process using prompt questions, modelling the kind of questions students should be asking themselves when they self-quiz.

5

CHECK FOR ACCURACY

After a short generative process, students should reveal the covered information to check the accuracy of their recall, in as much detail as is needed. It can be useful to repeat Steps 4 and 5 in an iterative loop, filling in gaps of knowledge, adding fluency each time until students feel confident that they can recall the information.

Over time, students should engage in the recall process with increasing time gaps after studying the knowledge organiser.

SECTIONS: WHY? | **WHAT?** | HOW?

118

BEHAVIOUR & RELATIONSHIPS | CURRICULUM PLANNING
EXPLAINING & MODELLING | QUESTIONING & FEEDBACK
PRACTICE & RETRIEVAL | MODE B TEACHING

REHEARSAL & PERFORMANCE

There are wide areas of the curriculum where a rehearse-perform-evaluate cycle is the most appropriate way to consider retrieval practice. This might be where students need to apply a technical skill or physical procedure. It can also be where a performance is the goal — such as in music or drama. It can also apply to giving detailed explanations of events, concepts or phenomena.

WALKTHRUs IN THIS SERIES

PRACTICE AND RETRIEVAL

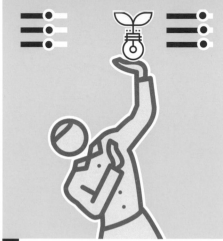

1

ESTABLISH THE CRITERIA FOR EXCELLENCE IN PERFORMANCE

Set out clear success criteria at the beginning, using rubrics and related exemplars as in **Set the Standard**.

Where creative, original outcomes are important, reinforce the diverse range of possible ways in which excellence might be achieved. Highlight key elements that are common tipping points for achieving next level success.

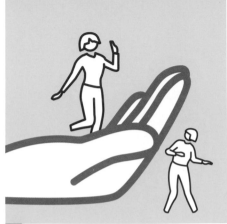

2

INITIATE LOW STAKES REHEARSAL

Give all students the opportunity to rehearse the performance, or explanation or demonstration of the skills in hand. At an early stage, allow students a period of private practice, away from scrutiny by the group so that the stakes are very low and they are essentially rehearsing for their own self-review. Use pairs or small groups to provide a source of feedback if needed.

3

GENERATE FEEDBACK

After each rehearsal engage students in a review process. What went well? What could be improved? Ideally this feedback would be self generated as this will have high impact. It could be generated from a Peer Critique process or the teacher can circulate during rehearsal giving advice. Ensure that feedback relates back to the established criteria as far as possible.

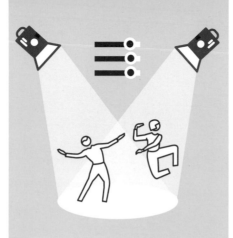

4

DELIVER THE PERFORMANCE

When ready, students should deliver a performance aiming to embed the feedback in achieving the success criteria. This might be done with pairs or groups working in parallel or by presenting to the whole class.

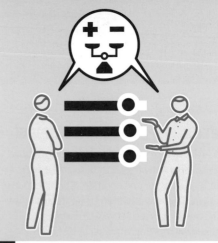

5

EVALUATE AND REPEAT

Compare students' performances — or their explanations or success in employing the skills — to the success criteria. Use questioning techniques such as **Check for Understanding** to establish whether students can see where they succeeded and where they can improve. Repeat Steps 2-4 to secure incremental improvements.

SECTIONS: WHY? | **WHAT?** | HOW?

120

BEHAVIOUR & RELATIONSHIPS | CURRICULUM PLANNING
EXPLAINING & MODELLING | QUESTIONING & FEEDBACK
PRACTICE & RETRIEVAL | MODE B TEACHING

PEER–SUPPORTED RETRIEVAL

As Wiliam et al suggest, a powerful formative assessment strategy is to 'activate learners as resources for one another'. A practical way of enacting this is to train students to engage in peer-supported retrieval. Essentially this means asking students to test each other's knowledge and to provide corrective feedback, supported by resources to ensure the feedback is accurate. By employing this strategy, teachers can significantly amplify the feedback students receive about the extent of their knowledge.

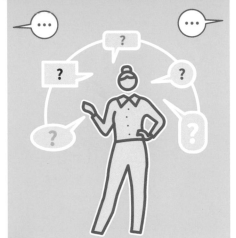

1

PROVIDE QUESTION AND ANSWER PROMPTS

Teach students how to ask each other questions by modelling them explicitly. This might include **Elaborative Interrogation** or **Using a Knowledge Organiser**. Part of the modelling should include the need to ask questions in a variety of forms and the goals of providing complete answers rather than fragments. For example: List all the noble gases. Which of these elements is not a noble gas? Which of these diagrams shows the atoms in a noble gas?

2

ALLOCATE CHECKING PARTNERS

As with any collaborative process, it is important to be explicit about expected behaviours. If you want students to quiz each other in pairs or to use a more elaborate group quiz structure, ensure that everyone has a clear role and learning goal. Manage the allocation of checking partners to prevent students engaging in ineffective group behaviours where more confident students dominate and less confident students give way.

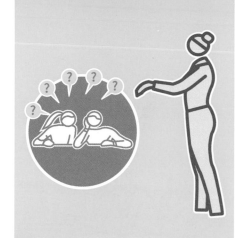

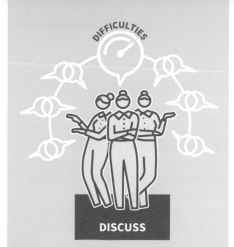

STUDENT 1 ASSESSES STUDENT 2

Invite one student in each pair to ask
a series of questions to check their
partner's knowledge. This could be in the
form of pre-prepared quiz questions; it
could be running through an extended
explanation, rehearsing the narrative in
a story, describing a series of processes;
adding labels to a diagram or flow chart;
completing some problem solving activities.

Student 1 should verify Student 2's answers,
confirming correct complete responses and
providing corrective feedback.

STUDENT 2 TESTS STUDENT 1

Swap the roles of the students and repeat
Step 3. It is likely, that Student 1, having
asked the questions in Step 3, will be in
a stronger position to give good answers
having just studied the material. Multiple
iterations of these steps can lead to
excellent fluency building.

DISCUSS COMMON DIFFICULTIES

Follow-up the paired quizzing process with
a discussion of common errors, difficulties
with recall, gaps in knowledge and
misconceptions. Instead of asking
"does everyone understand?", try to find
out who still does not understand.
Re-teach material as necessary.

Attempt | Develop | Adapt | **Practise** | Test

SECTIONS: WHY? | **WHAT?** | HOW?

122

BEHAVIOUR & RELATIONSHIPS | CURRICULUM PLANNING
EXPLAINING & MODELLING | QUESTIONING & FEEDBACK
PRACTICE & RETRIEVAL | MODE B TEACHING

WEEKLY & MONTHLY REVIEW

It's a strongly evidenced phenomenon that students secure stronger long-term recall if they engage in retrieval practice with a set of ideas after some time has passed. Rosenshine suggests that more effective teachers include periodic reviews of material learned in the last week or the last month to attenuate the rate of forgetting, supporting students to retain accurate schema in the long term. It also helps to make connections between ideas if a review samples a range of knowledge in an integrated manner. The challenge is to embed review processes into your routines whilst also keeping track of the path through the curriculum.

1

GENERATE STUDY RESOURCES

Provide or engage students in producing resources that will support them in building secure schema in the long term. This might include reading material, **Knowledge Organisers** or making structured notes in exercise books. It is much easier to engage in the evaluation part of a review if there are clear resources that the retrieval tasks relate to. This also supports students' independent study.

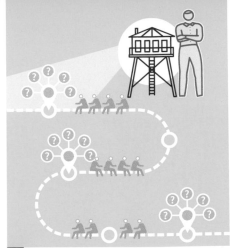

2

PLAN FOR SPACED PRACTICE

As well as planning lessons that take students forward through the curriculum, plan when you can take time to pause to look back over material that was explored previously. A weekly review might cover learning covered in the previous week; a monthly review might cover material covered in the previous month but these are only loose guides. You might choose to review material covered much longer ago. It can help to build in a routine time slot, for example a 15 minute slot once per week, to build a rhythm to your reviews.

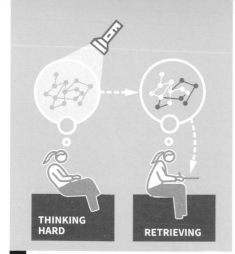

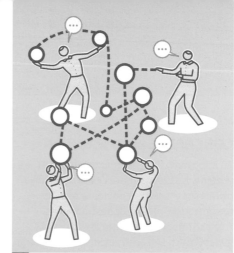

3

SET A RETRIEVAL PRACTICE ACTIVITY

Choose an appropriate retrieval practice activity to test students' recall of the previous learning. This could be any number of the strategies in our WalkThrus:

- **Quizzing** —with questions in varying formats
- **Peer–Supported Retrieval**
- **Elaborative Interrogation**
- **Rehearsal & Performance**

It could be through the use of mind-mapping, problem-solving or writing tasks that include elements of recall; reciprocal teaching, where students explore their recall by trying to explain the ideas to their peers.

4

EXPLORE GAPS AND ERRORS

Having engaged all students in checking their recall of all the relevant knowledge, take time to establish where the common gaps are. If students have forgotten things, give them time to reconsolidate their knowledge-base by re-examining the material; make a note to check again later. If they can no longer perform tasks or explain concepts, take time to re-teach the key ideas with a view to returning to it later. **Check for Understanding** across the class.

5

MAKE CONNECTIONS

Where possible, whilst reviewing previously learned material, show students how it connects to other topics they've covered including the current one. This helps to strengthen their wider schema-building, linking ideas together rather than making them seem isolated and disconnected.

SECTIONS: WHY? | **WHAT?** | HOW?

124

BEHAVIOUR & RELATIONSHIPS | CURRICULUM PLANNING
EXPLAINING & MODELLING | QUESTIONING & FEEDBACK
PRACTICE & RETRIEVAL | MODE B TEACHING

CONCRETE EXAMPLES

An important step in forming detailed schema, is students' capacity to make links from a set of specific concrete examples to some general rules or abstract ideas. It is also important to be able to illustrate general rules and abstract ideas with specific concrete examples. If material is studied and can be recalled both ways around, students form more secure schema for the ideas in hand and can be more fluent in subsequent recall. They will have developed a deeper understanding of the ideas.

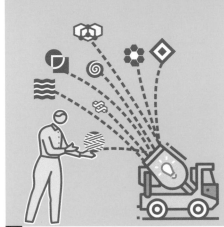

1

MAKE ABSTRACT–CONCRETE CONNECTIONS EXPLICIT

During instruction, make abstract-concrete connections a focus of your explanations. For example:

- Definitions of language features — metaphor, simile — and specific examples of each
- Patterns and trends in the Periodic Table — and specific examples with particular elements
- General properties of mountain formation and specific examples in different locations

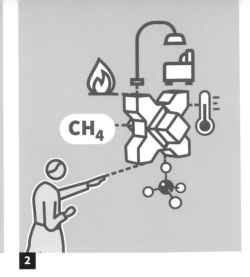

2

HIGHLIGHT A RANGE OF USEFUL CONCRETE EXAMPLES TO LEARN

Choose a defined set of concrete examples that typify the abstract ideas in hand. Provide resources explaining them so that students can include them in their retrieval activities:

- Methane, formula CH_4, the shortest chain hydrocarbon, has a low boiling point and is a gas at room temperature
- Jakarta in Indonesia has large slum areas and very wealthy neighbourhoods, typical of megacities in NEEs.

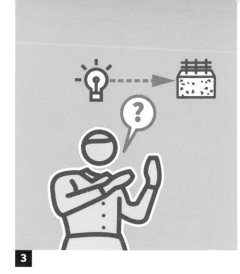

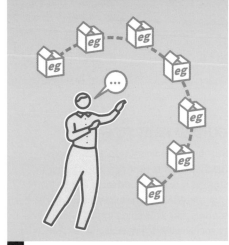

3

QUIZ ON CONCRETE EXAMPLES FOR A GIVEN ABSTRACT IDEA

Engage students in retrieval activities where the focus is to recall concrete examples of an abstract idea:

- Give an example of a metaphor.
- Give an example of a metal + acid reaction and state the products.
- Write a sentence using a fronted adverbial.
- Give an example of an empire and an emperor.

This could be part of **Peer–Supported Retrieval** or **Quizzing**.

4

QUIZ ON ABSTRACT IDEAS FOR GIVEN CONCRETE EXAMPLES

Invert Step 3 focusing retrieval on linking specific examples to a related general case or abstract idea:

- *"She glowed with pride, soaking up the applause"*. What language features are used?
- Your body keeps its temperature constant. What is this an example of? (Homeostasis).
- What is the medieval Trial by Fire an example of? (Trial by Ordeal).

This could be part of **Peer–Supported Retrieval** or **Quizzing**.

5

EXTEND THE RANGE OF EXAMPLES

Once students have succeeded in recalling the specific taught examples, continue to develop their range, adding more concrete examples of the abstract ideas encountered in the curriculum. Add them to the quizzing in Step 3 and Step 4, varying the type of questions used to test the depth of recall. Mix up the links — abstract to concrete and concrete to abstract and support students to check this type of recall in self-quizzing routines.

SECTIONS: WHY? | **WHAT?** | HOW?

126

BEHAVIOUR & RELATIONSHIPS | CURRICULUM PLANNING
EXPLAINING & MODELLING | QUESTIONING & FEEDBACK
PRACTICE & RETRIEVAL | MODE B TEACHING

GUIDED PRACTICE

Rosenshine makes it clear that effective teachers devote time to securing a high success rate when students begin to learn new material. This requires providing clear models and scaffolds, supporting students to succeed with new, challenging tasks. It also requires that teachers guide the early stages of practice, making sure that students are getting the details right, practising doing things right rather than doing things wrong. It involves taking time to re-teach material if it's clear that students are struggling too much or, conversely, moving students onto independent practice if they are gaining fluency quickly.

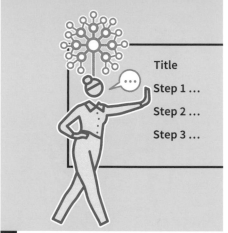

1

EXPLAIN AND MODEL THE NEW LEARNING

Introduce the new idea or skill using the range of **Explaining and Modelling** techniques. Take account of students' prior knowledge and confidence levels in highlighting the most important steps, common difficulties and misconceptions. Make it seem achievable.

2

SET SHORT TASK USING MODELLED KNOWLEDGE OR SKILL

Initiate the practice with a short task in which students are asked to follow the method or use the ideas that have been modelled. Where needed, keep the worked examples or exemplars in view as students engage in the practice.

WALKTHRUs IN THIS SERIES

PRACTICE AND RETRIEVAL

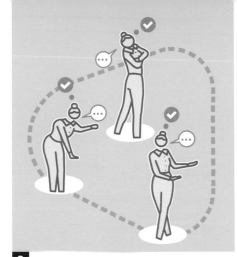

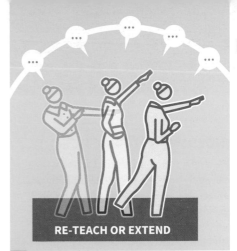

3

CIRCULATE ACTIVELY CHECKING FOR SUCCESS

As students practise, move around the teaching space looking for success with the modelled knowledge or skill. This is easier to do if you are walking amongst students rather than relying on observing from the front of the class and asking questions. Guiding practice involves engaging in individual feedback conversations as you circulate and gathering information to inform whole-class feedback.

4

CHECK FOR ERROR; AFFIRM SUCCESS

In order to build secure foundations with new learning, it's important to identify early successes, to reinforce the ideas or elements of performance to build confidence; it's also important to highlight key elements of weak performance or errors in understanding. Where these are common to the class, it is worth stopping to address the whole group (**Signal, Pause, Insist**) to restate or remodel aspects of the material in hand.

5

RE-TEACH OR EXTEND THE PRACTICE

As students are practising, it is natural for them to progress at different rates. Be vigilant in detecting students who are struggling and students who are flying through the material. In either case, initiate an appropriate response:

Re-teach or provide more modelled answers to reinforce first steps.

Or…

Extend the practice to include a wider range of examples or more challenging content.

Attempt | Develop | Adapt | Practise | Test

SECTIONS: WHY? | **WHAT?** | HOW?

128

BEHAVIOUR & RELATIONSHIPS | CURRICULUM PLANNING
EXPLAINING & MODELLING | QUESTIONING & FEEDBACK
PRACTICE & RETRIEVAL | MODE B TEACHING

INDEPENDENT PRACTICE

For students to reach the point where they can apply their learning independently with a level of fluency requires an element of often extensive practice. Independent practice supports the overlearning essential for students to develop the automaticity needed for fluent application and recall in future.

Moving from guided practice to independent practice is usually a continuum as teachers gradually reduce the level of guidance they provide. This might happen more rapidly for more confident students but independent practice is necessary for everyone and needs to be planned as part of a learning sequence.

1

SECURE GUIDED SUCCESS

Before students engage in independent practice, make sure that they have reached a certain level of confidence with the material during guided practice. If students are to succeed and build confidence, they need to be getting things mostly right, with practice aimed at improving fluency. If they are not ready, it can back-fire. Teacher judgement is critical here.

2

REMOVE SCAFFOLDS AND INITIATE PRACTICE

Set students tasks that use the same material featured during guided practice. This might be a straightforward repeat of near identical questions and activities to those that were previously modelled and supported with scaffolds. It could be an extension of those activities with increasing levels of challenge as students' fluency develops. It could involve **Collaborative Learning** activities where students practise within a structured peer-supported framework.

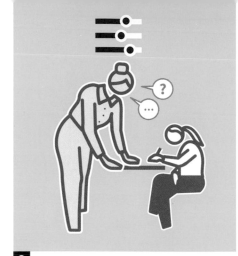

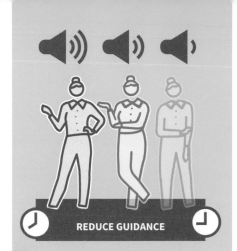

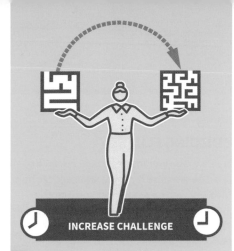

3

CHECK AND FEEDBACK

Evaluate the success of students' independent practice, providing feedback as needed to ensure that they are continuing to produce accurate responses and that their level of fluency is improving. Unchecked practice can result in drift from the original standards or a rate of improvement below the level expected.

4

REDUCE GUIDANCE OVER TIME

Use the strategy **Feedback That Moves Forward** avoiding the problem of SatNav syndrome. Make it explicit that a key element of students' independent practice is that they self-evaluate the quality of their performance or their success rate, using answer sheets or success criteria and exemplars. Fully independent performance will be achieved when students self-diagnose the gaps in their learning and take steps to address them independently. This needs to be built-in to the independent practice activities.

5

INCREASE CHALLENGE OVER TIME

As students' confidence and success rates improve as a result of their practice, direct them towards related tasks with a greater level of challenge. This could include attempting more synoptic questions, spanning multiple concepts; writing more extended pieces; attempting more difficult or more abstract problems; increasing the scope, pace or stamina in performance. Where possible map out the steps of increasing challenge in advance so students can take them independently.

Attempt | Develop | Adapt | Practise | Test

SECTIONS: WHY? | **WHAT?** | HOW?

130

BEHAVIOUR & RELATIONSHIPS | CURRICULUM PLANNING
EXPLAINING & MODELLING | QUESTIONING & FEEDBACK
PRACTICE & RETRIEVAL | MODE B TEACHING

BUILDING FLUENCY

Fluency is an important concept in learning. It refers to the capacity to recall knowledge from memory with minimal effort and a level of automaticity. This could relate to the physical aspects of playing sport or an instrument or performing a manual task; to reading and using language; to performing computational tasks and to retrieving factual knowledge. In nearly all cases, fluency is secured through repeated practice with a high success rate. The more often we complete a successful practice cycle, the more fluent we become in that area of learning.

1

DESIGN DRILLABLE ELEMENTS

Examine the knowledge and skills you want students to learn and break them down, identifying elements that can be performed repeatedly. Deconstruct complex tasks like speaking a language, playing a sport or writing an essay into a set of small, specific drillable elements. This will provide students with the building blocks of building fluency. Model each of the elements to your students as part of the instructional input.

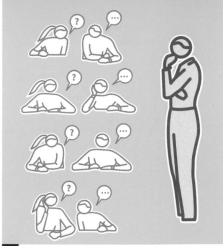

2

ENGAGE STUDENTS IN REPEATED LOW–STAKES PRACTICE

This will be very context specific but might include:

- Repeating words and phrases in a language.
- Repeating mathematical operations — times tables, number bonds — or algebraic procedures
- Repeating a mechanical/physical skill or process
- Repeating the explanation of an idea
- Repeating a quote or the sequence of a set of facts.

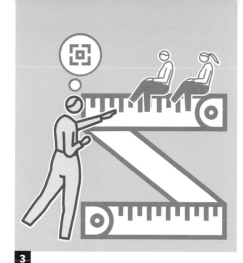

3

CHECK FOR ACCURACY AND PRECISION

While students perform their repeated practice routines, focus sharply on accuracy and precision. If it matters that words are pronounced correctly or that every single detail in a procedure in recalled or performed then highlight them as areas for students to work on in their practice.

4

INCREASE THE RANGE, PACE AND VARIETY

It's important that students develop flexible knowledge, not rigid knowledge. Make sure that practice routines include variety so that physical skills or knowledge recall activities require students to become agile in the way their fluency develops. After an initial level of fluency is achieved with the core task, add complexity, increasing the range of material incorporated into the tasks; increase the expectations of pace where appropriate and extend the difficulty of material that students are required to become fluent with.

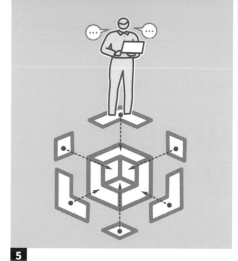

5

INTEGRATE THE ELEMENTS BACK INTO MORE COMPLEX TASKS

Once students are developing fluency in the component drills, put them back into their wider context by setting tasks combining the elements into a whole. This might mean:

- Playing a basketball match having worked on ball-handling drills
- Producing extended writing using the vocabulary and sentence structures from the drills
- Engaging in a conversation using newly acquired phrases in French
- Solving science problems using the equations involved in the rearranging equations drills.

Attempt | Develop | Adapt | Practise | Test

MODE B
TEACHING

In Tom's book *The Learning Rainforest*, he introduces the concept of Mode A and Mode B teaching to reflect the reality that many teachers typically balance different modes of teaching over time to add depth and variety of practice opportunities. Mode A teaching refers to the staple of teacher-led instructional teaching that forms the context for most of our WalkThrus. Mode B teaching is a broad collection of activities where, typically, students are given choices, engage in a more extended oral contributions and work collaboratively. This is very far from being an exhaustive set of ideas; it actually is just a very small sample of all the possibilities. The challenge for teachers is to weave Mode A and Mode B teaching into a cohesive whole, not in any one lesson, but over a whole unit of work.

SECTIONS: WHY? | **WHAT?** | HOW?

134   BEHAVIOUR & RELATIONSHIPS | CURRICULUM PLANNING
EXPLAINING & MODELLING | QUESTIONING & FEEDBACK
PRACTICE & RETRIEVAL | **MODE B TEACHING**

COLLABORATIVE LEARNING: GENERAL PRINCIPLES

It has been shown in various studies that collaborative learning can yield significant learning gains for students. In addition to social benefits, students can support each other in various forms of practice; they can share the cognitive load in engaging with new material and they can provide each other with trusted feedback. However, as Robert Slavin highlights, too often collaborative learning is delivered as unstructured 'group work' which can be ineffective. It's essential that the success of a group task depends on the success of each individual.

1

ESTABLISH INDIVIDUAL LEARNING GOALS

Establish the goals for each individual in a group in terms of the knowledge, skills and understanding they must acquire. This could be the same for all members or different for each individual. Crucially, the group task must support each individual to meet their learning goals.

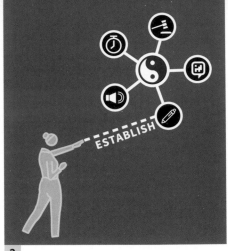

2

ESTABLISH A ROLE FOR EACH MEMBER OF THE GROUP

Engage groups in a process of establishing the specific role each individual will play. This might be something they can do themselves — agreeing roles between them — or the teacher might need to allocate the roles. This will be important so that one or two individuals do not dominate and nobody can opt out, becoming a passenger while everyone else does all the thinking and makes all the effort.

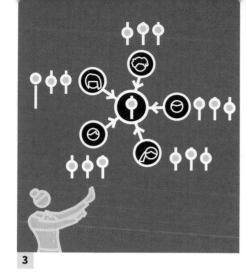

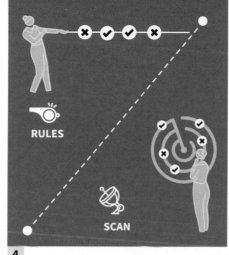

| 3 | 4 | 5 |

GROUP SUCCESS DEPENDS ON INDIVIDUALS' SUCCESS

Establish success criteria for the group which embeds the need for each individual to have met their learning goals. This could be achieved in various ways — e.g. each group needs to give equal time to each member in giving a presentation; each person's score in a knowledge test will be added up or must be above a minimum level; each participant must complete their piece of the problem in order to solve it.

MONITOR GROUP BEHAVIOURS

Establish ground rules for group behaviours and then monitor the group during their activities so that these are honoured. These might include taking turns to speak; making sure everyone's voice is heard; making sure that an individual's contributions are not taken over by others.

CHECK INDIVIDUAL AND GROUP OUTCOMES

On completing the task, review performance at both individual and group level.

Does everyone now have secure knowledge of the material? Have they all individually improved their fluency?

Did the group function well as a unit? Did the collaborative aspect succeed in supporting the success of individuals?

Attempt | Develop | Adapt | Practise | Test

SECTIONS: WHY? | **WHAT?** | HOW?

136

BEHAVIOUR & RELATIONSHIPS | CURRICULUM PLANNING
EXPLAINING & MODELLING | QUESTIONING & FEEDBACK
PRACTICE & RETRIEVAL | **MODE B TEACHING**

HOMEWORK AS GUIDED STUDY

It is common that, as students mature at school, they will increasingly be expected to prepare for assessments of various kinds. Sometimes they will have high stakes such as with public examinations. Among many other highly valuable purposes, homework can play an important role in training students to learn the skills and develop the habits needed to pursue a programme of study, deepening their knowledge, improving their fluency and confidence and generally enabling them to demonstrate their knowledge and understanding when needed.

1

ESTABLISH CLEAR LEARNING GOALS

Support students by establishing specific learning goals focused on specific sets of knowledge. This is especially important with younger or less confident students, with lower prior attainment. Set out exactly what knowledge, writing skills or practical skills they should be aiming to acquire through completing the homework tasks.

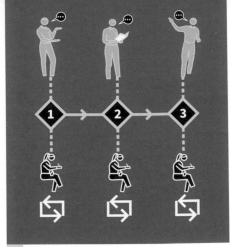

2

TEACH STUDY STRATEGIES EXPLICITLY

Identify all the study strategies you want your students to use and teach them all explicitly with modelling and practice opportunities during class time. This might include:

- Reading comprehension
- Making notes
- Summarising and mind-mapping
- **Retrieval Practice** methods
- Checking answers and making corrections.
- Practice routines.

3

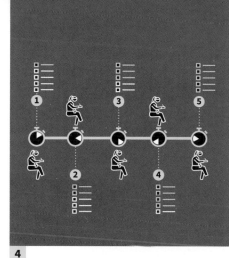

4

5

PROVIDE SUPPORTING RESOURCES

Ensure students have access to all the resources needed to complete a task. This will include texts, online tools, materials. Do not set tasks that depend on students' access to resources that cost money unless they are provided. Do not assume students have access to computers and the internet: check and make appropriate provision if needed. Remember that making resources available online is not the same as being sure that every student can and will access them.

SET STUDY TASKS WITH TIMELINES

For every task, provide guidance, resources and set a clear timeline. This will help students to learn to manage their time. Establish success criteria and set the standards for completed tasks using exemplars if appropriate to the task. Where needed, provide guidance about what students should do if they are stuck and how long they should be spending on the work.

EVALUATE SUCCESS

The key measure of success in a task will not be whether the task appears complete: it will be whether the students have met the learning goals. This could be assessed through various forms of retrieval practice or by looking at the quality of the work that has been produced. Peer and self-assessment methods are useful as part of a diet of feedback that includes some teacher feedback.

SECTIONS: WHY? | **WHAT?** | HOW?

138

BEHAVIOUR & RELATIONSHIPS | CURRICULUM PLANNING
EXPLAINING & MODELLING | QUESTIONING & FEEDBACK
PRACTICE & RETRIEVAL | **MODE B TEACHING**

ENQUIRY PROJECTS

In a rich curriculum diet, enquiry will be an important element over time even if it is not a routine approach. Once students have sufficient knowledge in an area, it is a powerful experience for them to learn how to pursue an enquiry process; learning to ask questions and then to pursue a process that leads them to some answers or to ask even more questions. This process needs structure and guidance and the appropriate level of prior knowledge. A project is typically more extended than pieces of work that can only be completed during lesson time.

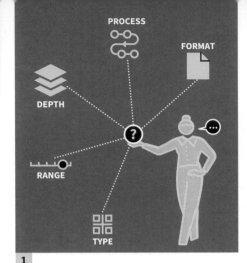

1

ESTABLISH THE ENQUIRY QUESTION

Give students a sense of the nature of the enquiry they are about to engage in. This might include the type, range and depth of knowledge, the nature of good questions, the general format of the enquiry process; the typical format of a report. Model the standards by showing some completed examples. From this they should construct a headline enquiry question to shape their project.

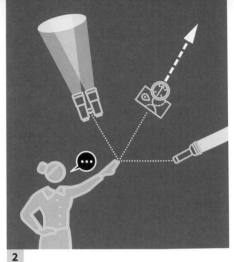

2

TEACH THE ENQUIRY SKILLS NEEDED IN ADVANCE

Identify the skills that students will need to pursue their enquiry. This will depend on the subject:

- Pre-requisite maths knowledge
- Measurement or observation techniques in science or geography
- Online research and filtering skills
- How to record and process data

Model all the individual skills you expect students to use and check for understanding. Engage in some guided practice of any complex skills.

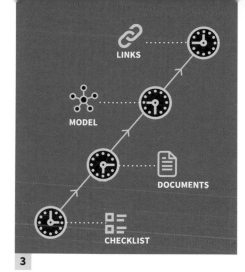

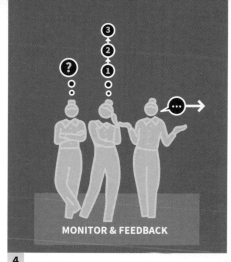

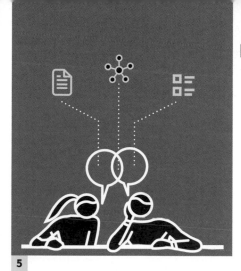

3

4

5

PROVIDE RESOURCES AND SCAFFOLDING; SET TIMEFRAMES

Make sure all students' have the resources to complete the enquiry process, especially if undertaken outside of class time. Use your knowledge of your students to provide them with the appropriate level of scaffolding so that they are guided enough to complete the task without being over-guided; this is an opportunity for students to practise thinking for themselves. Map out a timeframe for completing the enquiry project and any sub-components.

MONITOR AND PROVIDE INTERIM FEEDBACK

Monitor students' progress with their enquiry project at key points. This might include the very first stage of deciding on an interesting and realistic enquiry question. It might be at the data collection/information gathering or analysis stage. It is important to give **Feedback That Moves Forward** so the earlier you can identify areas to improve, the better.

SHOWCASE THE RESULTS

When students have completed their enquiry projects, provide a space to showcase their reports or give lesson time for students to talk about the work that they have done. This can be important element in focusing on what students understand rather than focusing on the production of artefacts. The goal of enquiry is to deepen understanding, not only to produce nice-looking artefacts, even if this is also important.

SECTIONS: WHY? | **WHAT?** | HOW?

140

BEHAVIOUR & RELATIONSHIPS | CURRICULUM PLANNING
EXPLAINING & MODELLING | QUESTIONING & FEEDBACK
PRACTICE & RETRIEVAL | **MODE B TEACHING**

OPEN RESPONSE TASKS

When students have explored a topic and accumulated a range of new knowledge, it can be very rewarding for them to showcase what they have learned in some format. The precise form of their response is not critical and it can provide a powerful opportunity for students to shape their learning experience if they are given the choice. This can result in a satisfying array of responses, personal to the students, that adds a richness you do not get if everyone makes the same thing. Even if you only do this once or twice a year, it can be very rewarding and valuable.

1

ENSURE PRE-REQUISITE KNOWLEDGE IS SECURE

Make sure that students have a good platform of knowledge on which to base their responses through the normal flow of lessons and formative assessment tasks. This will allow them to keep knowledge content in the forefront of their thinking when deciding on their presentational format. We don't want elaborate multimedia presentations without substance. We want detailed knowledge brought to life through the format.

2

AMPLIFY THE POSSIBILITIES

Give the instruction: *Showcase your knowledge of this topic in any form you choose*. Encourage diversity. Students could make:

- a video, a booklet, a website, write an essay or news report, produce a detailed summary poster, prepare a presentation, make some artefacts…

Show examples focusing on depth of knowledge and understanding in the material, not just visual features. Avoid only modelling one response as this will influence students' choices unduly.

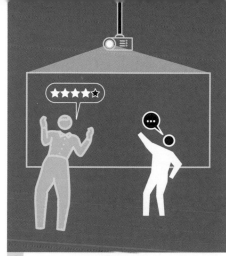

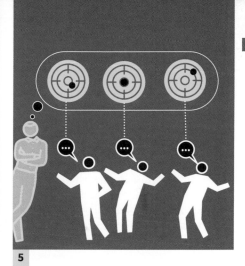

3

4

5

ENCOURAGE EXCELLENCE

Show a range of excellent examples so that students pitch high in their attempts to capture their learning. Discuss the features of excellence in contrasting exemplars. Promote three messages:

1) Be bold in making a choice about the format in which knowledge is presented.

2) Ensure that everything is done to a high standard.

3) Be prepared to explain all the knowledge content.

"Show your knowledge however you like; just dazzle me"

SHOWCASE THE RESULTS

Give time to showcase students' responses. A good reason to encourage diversity is so that you only have a few videos or PowerPoint presentations to show alongside other paper-based responses, creating an interesting range that can be explored in a time-efficient manner.

CHECK THAT DEEPER LEARNING GOALS ARE MET

Return to the core knowledge, keeping the focus on securing deeper learning. Use formative assessment tools to check that students can recall and apply the knowledge they've gathered. One good way to do this is to invite students to talk through their responses, taking questions from the teacher and the class. This helps to build speaking confidence at the same time.

Attempt | Develop | Adapt | Practise | Test

SECTIONS: WHY? | **WHAT?** | HOW?

142

BEHAVIOUR & RELATIONSHIPS | CURRICULUM PLANNING
EXPLAINING & MODELLING | QUESTIONING & FEEDBACK
PRACTICE & RETRIEVAL | **MODE B TEACHING**

ORACY: DEBATING

An excellent way to deepen students' understanding is to teach them how to engage in structured exchanges of ideas through one of the various forms of debating. This has the benefit of enhancing their confidence with speaking whilst also teaching them to consider the validity of alternative perspectives, how to make a persuasive argument and to respond to challenges.

WALKTHRUs IN THIS SERIES

MODE B TEACHING

1

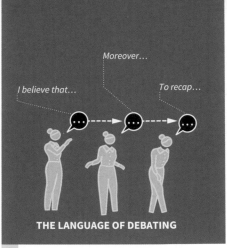

THE LANGUAGE OF DEBATING

2

ENSURE PRE-REQUISITE KNOWLEDGE IS SECURE

Make sure that the knowledge basis of any debate is taught securely. Debates based on poor knowledge can be counterproductive. Establish the parameters for a debate so that the process deepens students' knowledge and understanding. Examples might include:

- Would a nuclear power station or wind farm be a better solution in a given context?
- Is Macbeth a victim or the author of his own downfall?
- Is it ever morally acceptable to kill?

MODEL AND PRACTISE THE LANGUAGE OF DEBATING

Teach some key phrases that help to frame a debate exchange. Model them and engage students in practice:

- I believe that…
- In our opinion…Firstly…, secondly…
- What's more; moreover….
- There are two issues our opponents have failed to address, namely…
- Our opponents have claimed that… however…
- That may be the case, however
- To recap the main points…

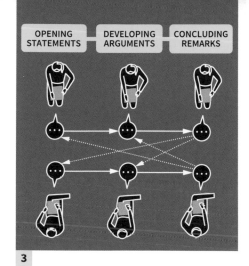

3

4

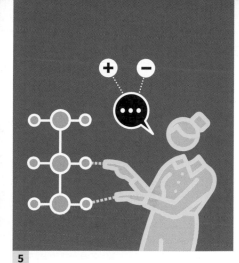

5

TEACH A SIMPLE DEBATE STRUCTURE

One to one: Students debating in pairs, exchanging ideas and practising the language.

Team debates: 2 vs 2 or 3 vs 3, each team allocated to propose or oppose a motion, with rehearsal time before the exchanges.

Multi-voice: A range of inputs making a case for a different position or proposal.

Give all debaters a role. Where necessary, introduce a moderator role, to monitor the exchange and keep timings.

RUN THE DEBATE FOLLOWING THE AGREED STRUCTURE

After an appropriate time for preparation, set up the debates. They can be run simultaneously or by using the rest of the class as an audience. The role of any observers can be to adjudicate or to express agree/disagree opinions based on the arguments presented. Keep to time so that students learn to prepare and perform within the discipline of a time structure, sharpening their case accordingly.

REVIEW THE CONTENT AND PROCESS

During and after the debates, provide instructional input and feedback to highlight the key learning points, to challenge obvious misconceptions, to separate fact from opinion and to ensure deeper understanding is consolidated.

Review the process of the debate so that lessons can be learned to improve subsequent debate activities and students' individual contributions.

SECTIONS: WHY? | **WHAT?** | HOW?

144

BEHAVIOUR & RELATIONSHIPS | CURRICULUM PLANNING
EXPLAINING & MODELLING | QUESTIONING & FEEDBACK
PRACTICE & RETRIEVAL | **MODE B TEACHING**

ORACY: TALK FOR WRITING

It can be very productive to engage students in a process of rehearsal prior to a writing task. It is largely true that, if you can't say something, you can't write it. Talk for writing is a process by which students run through their understanding, generating ideas and exploring possible lines of reasoning, retrieving key elements of knowledge and planning the overall structure for a writing task. The talk then informs the creation of a plan which, in turn, informs the actual writing.

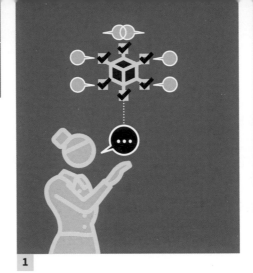

1

SET THE WRITING FOCUS AND ESTABLISH SUCCESS CRITERIA WITH EXEMPLARS

Before students begin, set out the focus of the discussion in terms of the general structure and content. This helps the talk for writing to have some depth, related to the material in hand. This can be more or less structured depending on the nature of the task. A creative writing task will need to be more open-ended than an analytical essay. Use the **Set the Standards** process.

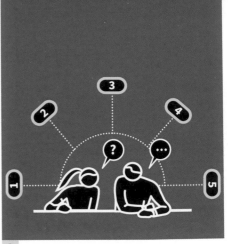

2

IN PAIRS, ASK STUDENTS TO TALK THROUGH THEIR IDEAS … STEP BY STEP

Initiate the pair discussions with some degree of structure:

- Explore all the possible ideas and concepts freely.
- Use **Elaborative Interrogation** to explore Why and How ideas are connected.
- Take turns to ask the questions about each other's ideas and plans for writing. Link this to **Deliberate Vocabulary Development** ensuring key words are practised.

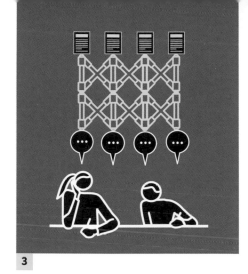

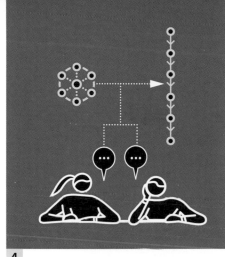

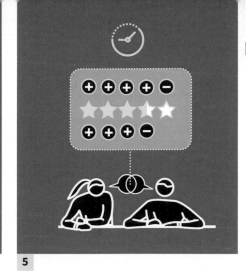

SCAFFOLD THE CONTENT OF THE TALK TO MATCH THE WRITING

Provide guidance so that the talk mirrors the demands of the writing task.

For an analytical essay, consider the key thesis, the supporting points and conclusion.

For a speech, consider the nature of the audience, how to embed some features of persuasive rhetoric.

For a story, consider the narrative structure, the use of dramatic devices, the beginning and ending.

ASK STUDENTS TO PRODUCE A PLAN

Make it explicit that the talk has to be purposeful. The initial product might be a free mindmap of the range of ideas explored. This can then be turned into a more ordered sequence that will form the basis of a plan. It can be useful to use structure headings to help organise the ideas. Ask students to review each other's plans and circulate to provide guidance and feedback at this developmental stage prior to the writing task.

GIVE TIME TO PRODUCE THE WRITING ACCORDING TO THE PLAN

Complete the sequence by setting the task of following through with the plan. Once complete, ask students to review each other's writing to verify whether it matched the range of ideas explored in their discussion. It is a fruitful discussion to compare what is said when talking compared to what is recorded in writing, refining the process for the next time it is used.

SECTIONS: WHY? | **WHAT?** | HOW?

146

BEHAVIOUR & RELATIONSHIPS | CURRICULUM PLANNING
EXPLAINING & MODELLING | QUESTIONING & FEEDBACK
PRACTICE & RETRIEVAL | **MODE B TEACHING**

ORACY: INSTRUCTIONAL INPUTS

In Shimamura's MARGE model, he suggests that engaging students in a process where they *"Think it, say it, teach it!"* can lead to significant gains for long-term recall. It is also a good personal development experience for students to address their peers to explain a concept or solve a problem. The task of preparing a set of instructions or explanatory steps is also a good challenging in terms of language and speech. It is possible to organise lessons so that all students are given this opportunity over time.

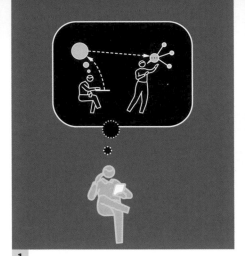

1

IDENTIFY MATERIAL FOR STUDENTS TO EXPLAIN

Identify specific set-piece instructional inputs that a student could deliver without too much support. It could be a concept in maths or science, a case study scenario in geography; a specific event, person or artefact in history or a particular section of a text in English. Alternatively find questions or problems for them to present model solutions to. They will need to have sufficient knowledge to do this or research skills to find the information in advance of the lesson.

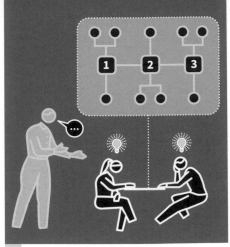

2

ALLOCATE INSTRUCTIONAL TASKS

Allocate a specific concept or question to an individual or pair of students and set them the task of preparing their instructional input on a specific date. Walk through the timeframe and content and check that they have the resources needed to prepare. Where needed, provide some guidance for the process e.g. not to read text from PowerPoint slides; to include diagrams and physical demonstration aids; to keep explanations short, broken down in small steps.

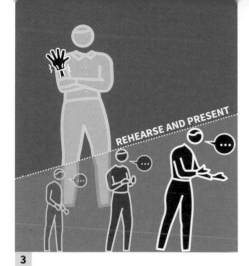

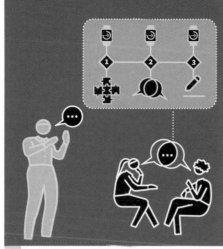

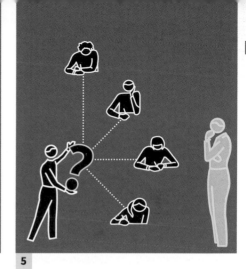

3

4

5

INVITE STUDENTS TO REHEARSE AND PRESENT MATERIAL

Give students the opportunity to practise their input or include this as a homework activity. Then, when ready, invite the students to address the class with their material. Stand at the back of the room to encourage them to project their voices clearly, making eye contact with students, not looking at the board. Where needed, give instructions to keep the class on track listening to their classmates' input.

INCLUDE TASKS FOR THE REST OF THE CLASS

A good instructional input will go beyond a presentation of information, developing into a mini lesson. Encourage students to design tasks for their class which follow from the input. This could be practice questions, problems, writing tasks or discussion tasks. It is important to clarify this in advance so that students all pay attention intently during the instructional input.

CHECK FOR RECALL AND UNDERSTANDING

Encourage your selected 'student teachers' to engage the class in Check for Understanding procedures, using various questioning or quizzing techniques. You should also feel free to interject, offering additional instructional input, correcting errors or misconceptions and generally supporting the student-teachers in what they are doing, all the while, checking for student understanding. .

Attempt | Develop | Adapt | Practise | Test

SECTIONS: WHY? | **WHAT?** | HOW?

148

BEHAVIOUR & RELATIONSHIPS | CURRICULUM PLANNING
EXPLAINING & MODELLING | QUESTIONING & FEEDBACK
PRACTICE & RETRIEVAL | **MODE B TEACHING**

INDEPENDENT LEARNING: PRE–READING

Several commentators have suggested that the concept of 'flipped learning' probably began when books were invented. When students are ready and have the resources, it is possible for teachers to ask them to read certain sections of the material in advance of a lesson. This frees up the teacher from using lesson time to impart information and puts the emphasis more on checking for understanding, exploring misconceptions and applying the knowledge to new contexts. The more students do this, then the more routine it becomes and the better they get at doing it. It also creates a sense of ownership and responsibility.

1

CONSTRUCT STRUCTURED COMPREHENSION OR RESEARCH TASKS

Make sure that pre-reading tasks are conducted to the appropriate level of depth by setting students specific goals. This could be to find certain words and concepts in order to explore their meaning; it could be to gain an overview of the narrative of events; it could be to generate structured summarised notes.

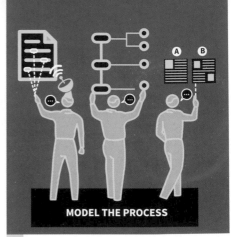

2

MODEL THE COMPLETION OF THE TASKS

While establishing the process, model each aspect of the pre-reading task completion explicitly. Show students how you skim and scan text to find key words and definitions; show them how to organise notes. Set the standard for the type of record you expect students to keep of what they have learned from their pre-reading task, using standard formats that can be used often so that they become part of students' study routines.

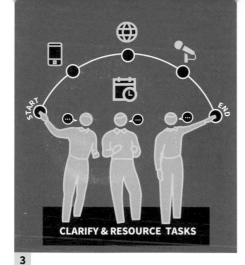

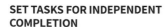

CLARIFY & RESOURCE TASKS

INVITE RESPONSES

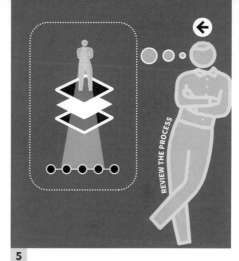

REVIEW THE PROCESS

3

SET TASKS FOR INDEPENDENT COMPLETION

Give students the tasks to complete relating to specific concepts or texts and set a timeframe and date for the lesson where they need to come ready to share what they have learned. As with **Homework as Guided Study**, ensure that all students have access to all the materials and technology they need.

4

INVITE RESPONSES AND CHECK FOR UNDERSTANDING

Invite students to present the fruits of their independent reading tasks. This could be:

- **Cold Calling:** Selecting students to give an extended expositions of the key points.
- **Paired Presentations:** Ask students to pool ideas and then present.
- **Retrieval Challenges:** Set generative quizzes and questions to test the depth of reading.
- **Problems and Errors:** Provide problems and mock responses containing errors, inviting students to solve them correctly.

5

REVIEW THE PROCESS AND REPEAT

This is an area of independent study that needs early guidance before students become adept at selecting the right information for note-taking and learn at the level of depth and rigour expected. Review the success of each episode of pre-reading, returning to exemplars and modelling as needed and give students further direction as needed.

Attempt | Develop | Adapt | Practise | Test

HOW?

WALKTHRUs FOR DEVELOPMENT

01

WHY?
REASONS FOR
THE WALKTHRUs

PAGE 08

02

WHAT?
THE WALKTHRU
SERIES

PAGE 32

03

The How section includes a set of guides for teachers and leaders regarding the implementation of WalkThrus as a tool for teacher development. This includes the ADAPT strategy, the use of a WalkThru in an instructional coaching scenario and the more general organisation of effective professional learning.

The WalkThrus might be self explanatory on first reading but the way ideas translate into improved practice is complex so it is essential that teachers and leaders think hard about how to engineer professional learning processes that are effective and sustained.

SECTIONS: WHY? | WHAT? | **HOW?**

152 | **ADAPT** | INSTRUCTIONAL COACHING | OBSERVATIONS | UNSEEN OBSERVATIONS | RUNNING CPD CYCLES | SOLVE THE LEARNING PROBLEMS

A|D|A|P|T

A key part of our thinking behind WalkThrus is that they are deliberately generic and context free. We are committed to the idea that a WalkThru is a not a rigid recipe or checklist that must be adhered to. It is only ever a reference point for reflection or to support coaching and feedback discussions.

At the bottom-right of every WalkThru page you will find the same message repeated: Attempt: Develop: Adapt: Practise: Test — spelling out ADAPT. It is essential the teachers ADAPT the WalkThrus so that they take form in their very specific contexts — with their subject; their students; their classroom.

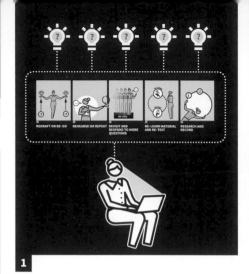

1

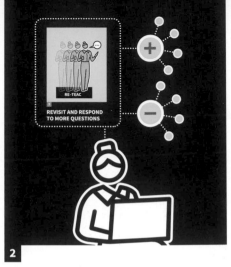

2

ATTEMPT

Take one WalkThru at a time. Run through the five steps and attempt to apply them to your context. You might do this as a mental WalkThru process; you might try it out in a real classroom context to establish whether the steps make sense. Evaluate the success of your attempt. Do the steps work? Are they the right sequence? Is anything missing? Would you do it differently?

DEVELOP

Add additional details to the steps so that they are more fine-grained; more precise; more detailed in relation to your subject content or the make-up of a specific class.

There are no *silver bullets* in teaching… Each teacher has to learn how to create the conditions that will produce the results they desire.

VIVIANE ROBINSON

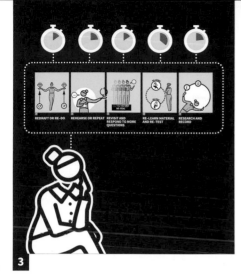

ADAPT

Change the WalkThru so that it works better for you. You might want to change the order; spend longer on certain steps than others; create more loops back to the beginning or link to other strategies more directly or call the steps different names. As far as possible, do this collaboratively with colleagues to maintain a shared understanding of the technique under discussion.

PRACTISE

Put your adapted WalkThru into action. If you are going embed it into your routine practice, you will need to practise the steps, evaluating their success as you go, making small adjustments of emphasis and timing until you feel that the strategies are working well.

TEST

The effectiveness of a strategy is really measured by the impact it has on student learning. To evaluate your impact you may gain insights from your subjective sense of how things feel but for a more rigorous analysis, you will also need to test it in a systematic, objective manner. This might include examining the quality of student work and the outcomes of various formative assessments. Continue to ADAPT the WalkThru in light of the insights you gain.

SECTIONS: WHY? | WHAT? | **HOW?**

154 ADAPT | **INSTRUCTIONAL COACHING** | OBSERVATIONS |
UNSEEN OBSERVATIONS | RUNNING CPD CYCLES |
SOLVE THE LEARNING PROBLEMS

INSTRUCTIONAL COACHING

Coaching is not new. It's been around for millennia. But since the 1980s, a new form of coaching has developed that grew of out of the previous decade's human potential movement (Brock 2014).

Executive, or life, coaching first entered the business world soon after. Then, some years later, was adopted in education as part of a CPD strategy.

But the core notion of the coach not having any technical knowledge of the activity being coached began to be questioned. Especially when the evidence for such an approach was becoming embarrassingly absent (Sams 2019).

WHERE IT BEGAN

Jim Knight, at Kansas University, has been a pioneer in the evolution of Instructional Coaching in education for over two decades. His documented work with schools is invaluable in charting the move away from the executive/life coaching model.

JIM KNIGHT

> Instructional coaches partner teachers to help them incorporate research–based instructional practices into their teaching.

THE APPROACH

This comparison opposite shows how Instructional Coaching is midway between the two better–known models of coaching.

EXECUTIVE/LIFE COACHING	INSTRUCTIONAL COACHING	SPORTS COACHING
FACILITATIVE	**DIALOGICAL**	**DIRECTIVE**
Coaches work from the assumption that the teacher already knows what to do	Teacher and coaches work together as partners	Coaches work from the assumption that teachers don't know what to do

THE PROCESS

Instructional Coaching is not designed solely for teaching the basics to the newly qualified. It is effective for all teachers.
What might differ are the different roles each group adopts in the analysis of their needs. The partnership approach implies a sharing of perception. Then, in the learning phase, the Instructional Coach's knowledge of teaching techniques takes centre stage.

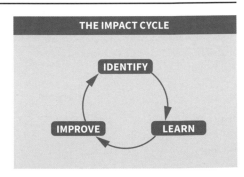
THE IMPACT CYCLE

IDENTIFY

IMPROVE

LEARN

THE NEED FOR KNOWLEDGE

Jim Knight is very clear on the role of pedagogical knowledge in the make–up of an Instructional Coach (IC).

He says (Knight 2007) that:

"ICs run the risk of being inefficient if they don't have a repertoire of effective practices to share with teachers." (p.177)

For that to happen, ICs need to…

"read, reread, and read again the instructors' manuals or research articles that describe the teaching practices they will be sharing." (p.114)

That, of course, informs the IC but doesn't prepare their communication of it to teachers. They, therefore, need to have…

"prepared one-page summaries (called 'Strategies at a Glance') of the teaching practices they share to make it easier for people to learn quickly about the interventions." (p.190)

Lastly, Knight quotes Csikszentmihalyi

"Ideas are most likely to survive and spread if they are easier to use and more powerful than the memes they are replacing."
(Knight p.190; Csikszentmihalyi 1993)

THE WALKTHRU SUPPORT

WalkThrus were designed specifically with these issues in mind.

All coaches — Instructional or not — have an evidence-informed curated index of techniques that serve all age phases, subjects and groups of students.

Busy teachers don't have the time to read all the necessary material. Nor should they reinvent the wheel — on their own — in this way. Coaches and teachers have a right to this information directly and efficiently.

We're confident that giving teachers access to our catalogue of WalkThrus, designed for effective communication and learning, would provide a powerful support for Instructional Coaching.

Easier, practical, powerful, attractive — the WalkThrus are designed for busy teachers wanting to improve quickly and effectively.

SECTIONS: WHY? | WHAT? | **HOW?**

156 ADAPT | INSTRUCTIONAL COACHING | **OBSERVATIONS** |
UNSEEN OBSERVATIONS | RUNNING CPD CYCLES |
SOLVE THE LEARNING PROBLEMS

OBSERVATIONS

Being coached is an act of faith — trust is paramount. Assuming teacher autonomy in the choice of development route, the building of a shared understanding of the selected WalkThru with teacher and observer is critical for coaching success.

And in the very process of studying and explaining the technique step by step, the teacher rapidly learns to internalise the actions needed for success. Familiarity builds from the very first glance.

| Mental practice alone produced about two thirds of the benefits of actual practice. | Sitting quietly, without moving, and picturing yourself performing a task successfully from start to finish improves performance significantly. |

CHIP & DAN HEATH

SELECT

1

SELECT A WALKTHRU

Reading through and selecting a WalkThru positively advances your learning. Simply looking and imagining yourself walking through the steps helps assimilate the information — in body and mind. Such embodied cognition plays an important part in learning new skill.

EXPLAIN

2

TALK THROUGH THE WALKTHRU

As you explain your choice of technique to your coach, you explain it in your own words, furthering your familiarity. Your coach observer — respecting your autonomous choice — starts to become more familiar with its details.

You may have a conversation where you discuss how the technique might be adapted to suit your context.

Arriving at this degree of shared understanding reinforces your learning and gives you confidence that the observation will be framed entirely through this sequence.

FRAME

3

REVIEW

4

PLAN

5

OBSERVE THROUGH THE FRAME OF THE WALKTHRU

As you start executing the technique, you do so with the reassurance that your observer will be viewing the scene and your actions entirely through the frame of your selected WalkThru. There will be no surprise "gotcha!" moments.

By observing through this frame, your coach observer will have their perceptions shaped in a behavioural structure. This will mean you can expect precise and concrete feedback that directly relate to the five steps and their descriptions.

REVIEW WITH THREE POINT COMMUNICATION

With the WalkThru placed in front of you both, you and your coach observer sit side by side, not face to face. This allows the coach to make their feedback directly to the WalkThru, not to your face. Doing so, puts a distance between them, the messenger, and their message.

This Three Point Communication is designed to reduce any personal aspect and maintain an objective perspective. As a result, it is far easier to keep the accent on the teaching and not the teacher.

PLAN AND AGREE NEXT MOVES

You and your coach may decide to continue working on the specific skill of this WalkThru. In this case, you will design adaptations based on the feedback, and prepare to be ready for the next observation and feedback cycle. Or, you may decide to move onto a new WalkThru, in which case you repeat the process once more anew. But, in general, there will be several cycles as you fine-tune your execution and move the skill rapidly into automatic mode, freeing up working memory for more responsive teaching.

SECTIONS: WHY? | WHAT? | **HOW?**

158

ADAPT | INSTRUCTIONAL COACHING | OBSERVATIONS |
UNSEEN OBSERVATIONS | RUNNING CPD CYCLES |
SOLVE THE LEARNING PROBLEMS

UNSEEN OBSERVATIONS

Researcher Matt O'Leary created the practice of Unseen Observations as he was acutely aware of how the presence of an observer alters the dynamics of a classroom.

In Unseen Observations all the important features of observations take place — planning, discussing, reviewing and back to planning — but without there being an observer present. Teachers meet to plan and review anytime before and after the targeted lesson, often at the start and end of a normal teaching day.

One of the central aims…is to encourage the teacher to engage in a process of reflection and analysis.

MATT O'LEARY

SELECT & AGREE

1

AGREE A WALKTHRU WITH A PARTNER

Select — either together or separately — a WalkThru technique you both want to learn. Your colleague doesn't have to teach the same subject or age phase. There are advantages to having both similar and dissimilar teaching contexts.

Read through the WalkThru several times, imagining yourself in the place of the illustrated teacher figures. Acknowledge that this is your first rehearsal, albeit an internal, mental one.

ADD YOUR CONTEXT

2

TALK THROUGH YOUR CONTEXT FOR THE WALKTHRU

When meeting up — maybe on the morning of the Unseen Observation — talk through the A | D | A | P | T process. Explain the reasoning behind your small changes you've thought of. Similarly, listen to your colleague's explanations and question the reasoning if you think it helpful.

Agree to meet at the end of the day for a review of how the WalkThru went.

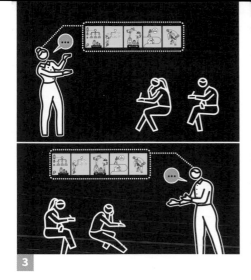

3

EXECUTE YOUR WALKTHRU PLANS — UNSEEN BY AN OBSERVER

Have a normal teaching day. At the lesson you have targeted to trial the WalkThru technique, simply execute the five steps you have already studied and mentally rehearsed.

4

REVIEW, WITH PARTNER, YOUR EXECUTION OF THE WALKTHRU

Meet up with your colleague at the end of the day. In turn, each of you talk through the WalkThru and its execution. Compare your anticipated impact — including the contextual tweaks — with what actually happened. Explore these discrepancies to highlight any faulty reasoning in your plans.

Use the behavioural descriptors and visuals of the WalkThru to frame the conversation around actions and how they can be specifically improved.

5

PLAN FURTHER ADAPTATIONS BASED ON YOUR REFLECTION AND DISCUSSIONS

When both of you have reviewed your WalkThru execution, focus on co-planning improvements. Using what you have learned from your evaluation of your previous planning and its execution, highlight areas that could benefit from some amendments. These will form the basis of your next Unseen Observation, maybe in the following week.

SECTIONS: WHY? | WHAT? | **HOW?**

160 ADAPT | INSTRUCTIONAL COACHING | OBSERVATIONS |
UNSEEN OBSERVATIONS | **RUNNING CPD CYCLES** |
SOLVE THE LEARNING PROBLEMS

RUNNING CPD CYCLES

The research into effective professional learning supports the importance of having a rhythm of regular sessions, ideally with an iterative cyclical structure. This allows reflection on problems and successes since the last session, exploration of new ideas and strategies and action planning for the next cycle.

It's important for strategies to be supported by a conceptual model so the reasons for them are understood and that teachers focus on a few ideas for a sustained period.

> As important as the amount of time is the kind of time … having it little and often, regular and built into the rhythm of the school day.

PHILLIPA CORDINGLEY

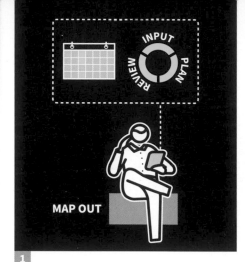

1

MAP OUT THE CYCLES

Within the timeframe available, map out when each session will take place so that everyone involved can visualise successive cycles of review, input and action planning. In any session it is important to know when the next one will be so that participants can put a timeframe around their professional learning process. Without this, sessions can fall into the 'hit and hope' trap, reducing their impact.

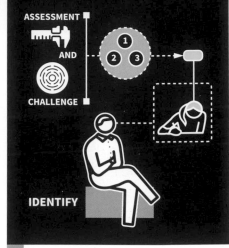

2

IDENTIFY PRIORITIES BASED ON STUDENTS' NEEDS

Given limited time, it's important to focus activities around the learning challenges that students face, rather than teachers' preferences and personal needs, in order to maximise the impact. Use assessment information to highlight the key curriculum areas where groups of individuals experience challenges and use the **Solve the Learning Problems** approach. During sessions keep focused on how the process will help to address those specific problems.

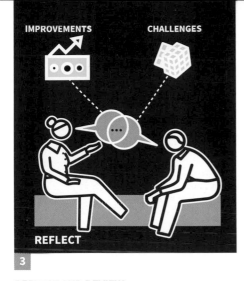

REFLECT

3

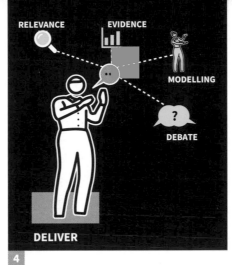

DELIVER

4

PLAN

5

REFLECT AND REVIEW

Begin each session with a review of progress since the last one. This can involve teachers discussing in pairs or trios, allowing everyone to contribute, rather than in a large group. The purpose is to provide a forum for noting where improvements are being made and airing ongoing challenges. Sharing both elements helps teachers to continue the problem-solving thinking, to gain peer support through shared experience or to share alternative approaches. It's important that the spirit of this process is open and honest rather than seeking to continually celebrate how successful everything has been.

DELIVER INPUTS: SEEK EVIDENCE; MODEL STRATEGIES

Useful new learning in a CPD session will ideally have some or all of these features:

- Relevance to the learning challenges teachers are seeking to tackle.
- An evidence base either from research, an analysis of assessment information or sampling student work.
- Active modelling of strategies, clarifying processes, putting them in the context that people are working in.
- Opportunities to debate, question and challenge creating alignment with personal values and learning models.

PLAN NEXT STEPS

Before each session ends, teachers should consider the detail of their next steps, continuing to practise or deploying new learning in the context of the classes they are going to teach. It is useful to make some form of commitment to this so that the next cycle will be approached with a sense of purpose and the appropriate level of intensity needed to secure positive impact. It can be important to remain focused on a few tightly defined areas rather than seeking to attempt too much. Peer observation and other feedback elements should be planned into the cycle as far as possible.

SECTIONS: WHY? | WHAT? | **HOW?**

162

ADAPT | INSTRUCTIONAL COACHING | OBSERVATIONS |
UNSEEN OBSERVATIONS | RUNNING CPD CYCLES |
SOLVE THE LEARNING PROBLEMS

SOLVE THE LEARNING PROBLEMS

In designing the content for the Teaching WalkThrus, we have focused on strategies that commonly offer solutions to tackling students' learning problems. This emphasis can be a much more productive and healthy approach compared to focusing directly on teachers' performance. In any class there will be students who find it more difficult than others, who do not score full marks on the assessments. What are the problems they experience? This is where to begin when looking for strategies.

REVIEW STUDENT PERFORMANCE

Formative assessments, reviews of student work and formal summative test information will point to the areas where students experience the greatest success and the greatest challenges. Use this information to consider what might need to be done or improved in terms of the way lessons are planned and executed.

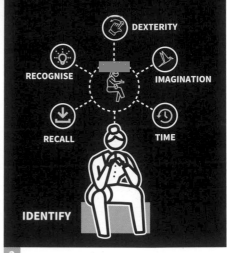

IDENTIFY PRECISE POINTS WHERE STUDENTS STRUGGLE OR CAN IMPROVE

The more precise teachers can be, the more accurate the selection of strategies can be. In any task that students undertake, the learning problems might relate to:

- Recall and understanding of key concepts
- Fluency in applying knowledge
- Recognising what is being asked from the questions
- Physical dexterity and confidence with procedures and skills
- Producing imaginative or sophisticated responses
- Performing under time constraints

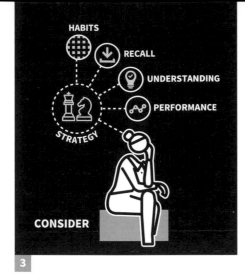

CONSIDER

3

e.g. WALKTHRU: FEEDBACK AS ACTIONS

SELECT

4

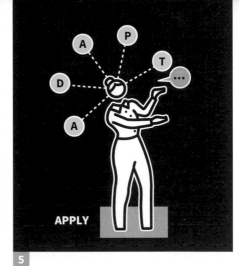

APPLY

5

CONSIDER STRATEGIES THAT BRIDGE THESE GAPS

Match strategies to the learning problems e.g.:

- Habits and routines ▸ **Behaviour and Relationships**
- Fluency and recall ▸ **Weekly and Monthly Review**
- Understanding ▸ **Explaining and Modelling**
- Quality of performance ▸ **Independent Practice**

It is rarely a case of introducing a new element into a teacher's practice. It is more likely to be a question of increasing the intensity, or teaching with more frequent cycles of feedback and improvement.

SELECT WALKTHRUs RELEVANT TO DELIVERING THE STRATEGIES

Use the menu of options from the WalkThrus to identify specific sets of steps to take in addressing the students' learning problems. It is better to focus on one of these at a time. Consider using the **Instructional Coaching** and **Unseen Observation** approaches.

APPLY THE A|D|A|P|T PROCESS

Attempt. Have a go to see how it works initially

Develop. Add additional steps for more precision.

Adapt. Make sense of the WalkThru for the subject or class context.

Practise: Take time to rehearse each of the steps, overcoming initial challenges and increasing fluency.

Test: Evaluate the impact of any WalkThru using objective information. Are the learning problems being solved?

Amasiatu, A.,N.	2013	**Mental Imagery Rehearsal As A Psychological Technique To Enhance Sports Performance**	Educational Research International
Berger, R.	2003	**An Ethic of Excellence**	Heinemann, Portsmouth, NH
Brock, V., G.	2014	**Sourcebook of Coaching History (2nd ed)**	Self-published
Bransford, J.	2000	**How People Learn**	National Academy Press, Washington
Cairo, A.	2013	**The Functional Art**	New Riders
Caviglioli, O.	2019	**Dual Coding With Teachers**	John Catt Educational, Woodbridge
Cordingley, P.		**Interview with Danielle Toon, Evidence for Learning**	https://evidenceforlearning.org.au/assets/Collateral/TRANSCRIPT-with-Philippa-Cordingley-from-CUREE.pdf
Cowan, N.	2001	**The Magical Number 4 in Short-Term Memory: A Reconsideration of Mental Storage Capacity**	Behavioural and Brain Sciences, 24, pp.87-114
Education Endowment Foundation	2018	**Metacognition and Self-Regulated Learning – Guidance Report**	London
Fiorella, L. & Mayer, R.	2015	**Learning As A Generative Activity**	Cambridge University Press, New York
Gawande, A.	2009	**The Checklist Manifesto: How To Get Things Right**	Henry Holt & Co., New York
Grinder, M.	2006	**Charisma: The Art of Relationships**	Michael Grinder & Associates
Heath, C. & Heath, D.	2007	**Made To Stick**	
Knight, J.	2007	**Instructional Coaching**	Corwin & LearningForward
Leahy, S. et al	2005	**Student Self Grading: Perception vs Reality**	American Journal of Educational Research, vol.3, No. 4, 450-455
Lemov, D.	2015	**Teach Like A Champion 2.0**	Hoboken, NJ: John Wiley & Sons
Lemov, D.et al	2012	**Practice Perfect**	Jossey-Bass, San Francisco
Lunzer E. & Gardner, K.	1984	**Learning From the Written Word**	Oliver & Boyd, Edinburgh

Mijksenaar, P. & Westendorp, P.	1999	**Open Here: The Art of Instructional Design**	Joost Elffers Books, New York
Modley, R. (ed)	2007	**1100 Pictorial Symbols**	Dover Publications, New York
Neurath, O.	1931	**Bildstatistik nach Wiener Methode**	Die Volksschule, 27. Reprinted in O. Neurath, Gesammelte bildpadagogische Schriften, Holder-Pichler-Tempsky, Vienna, Austria
O'Leary, M.	2014	**Classroom Observations**	Routledge, London
Polanyi, M.	2009 (1966)	**The Tacit Dimension**	University of Chicago, Chicago
Robinson, V.	2003	**Teachers as Researchers: A Professional Necessity?**	Set, vol. 1, 27-29
Rosenshine, B.		**Principles of Instruction**	International Academy of Sciences, http://www.ibe.unesco.org/fileadmin/user_upload/Publications/Educational_Practices/EdPractices_21.pdf
Sherrington, T.	2017	**The Learning Rainforest**	John Catt Educational, Woodbridge
Sherrington, T.	2019	**Rosenshine's Principles in Action**	John Catt Educational, Woodbridge
Shimamura, A.	2018	**MARGE: A Whole-Brain Learning Approach for Students and Teachers**	
Sibbert, D.	2011	**Visual Teams**	Wiley, New Jersey
Sims, S.	2019	**Four Reasons Instructional Coaching is Currently the Best-Evidenced Form of CPD**	https://samsims.education/blog-2/
Sweller, J. et al	2011	**Cognitive Load Theory**	Springer, New York
Weinstein, Y. et al	2018	**Understanding How We Learn: A Visual Guide**	Routledge, London
Wiliam, D.	2012	**Embedding Formative Assessment**	Solution Tree Press, Bloomington
Wiliam, D.	April 2014	**Establishing Successful Teacher Learning Communities: Lessons Learned (presentation slides)**	International Conference on Assessment for Learning, Fredericton
Willingham, D.	2009	**Why Don't Students Like School?**	Jossey-Bass, San Francisco

Look out for more **WALKTHRU** *features…*

Our dedicated website: www.walkthrus.co.uk with guidance, blogs and shop

Subscription packages for schools and colleges providing book discounts, web-based editions to access from any device and annual updates to training slides and future releases of WalkThrus Volume 2 and 3

TEACHING
WALKTHRUs
#2

TEACHING
WALKTHRUs
#3

Training slides and supporting materials for running your own CPD sessions

The WalkThrus online shop with materials to support coaching sessions and a range of t-shirt designs — with a share of profits donated to charity